Also from Westphalia Press
westphaliapress.org

Saber & Scroll

Volume 6
Issue 1
Winter 2017

Editor-in-Chief,

Michael Majerczyk

WESTPHALIA PRESS
An imprint of Policy Studies Organization

Saber & Scroll: Volume 6, Issue 1, Winter 2017

Westphalia Press
An imprint of Policy Studies Organization
1527 New Hampshire Ave., NW
Washington, D.C. 20036
info@ipsonet.org

ISBN-13: 978-1-63391-891-7
ISBN-10: 1-63391-891-2

Cover design by Jeffrey Barnes:
jbarnesbook.design

Daniel Gutierrez-Sandoval, Executive Director
PSO and Westphalia Press

Updated material and comments on this edition
can be found at the Westphalia Press website:
www.westphaliapress.org

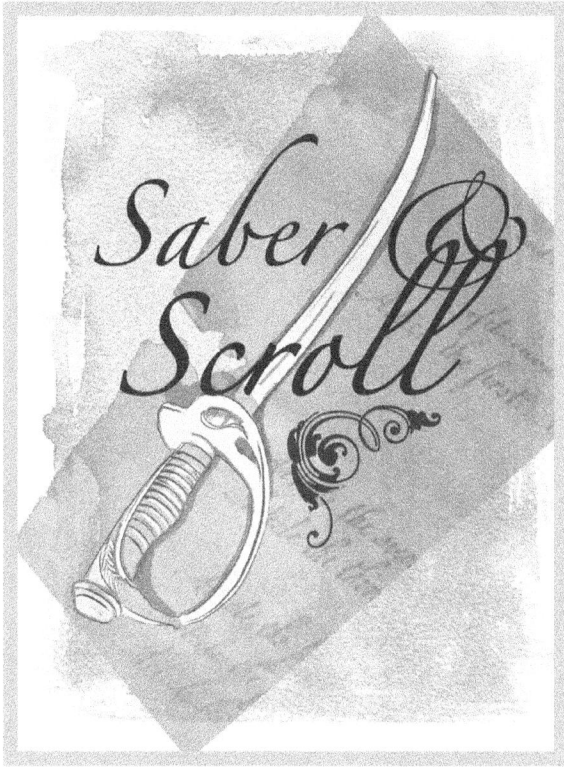

Saber and Scroll Journal

Volume VI Issue I

Winter 2017

Saber and Scroll Historical Society

Logo Design: Julian Maxwell

Cover Design: *Joan at the coronation of Charles VII*, oil on canvas by Jean Auguest Dominique Ingres, c. 1854. Currently at Louvre Museum.

Members of the Saber and Scroll Historical Society, the volunteer staff at the Saber and Scroll Journal publishes quarterly.

saberandscroll.weebly.com

Journal Staff

Editor in Chief

Michael Majerczyk

Copy Editors

Anne Midgley, Michael Majerczyk

Content Editors

Tormod Engvig, Joe Cook, Mike Gottert, Kathleen Guler,
Michael Majerczyk, Anne Midgley,
Jack Morato, Chris Schloemer, Christopher Sheline

Proofreaders

Aida Dias, Tormod Engvig, Frank Hoeflinger, Anne Midgley,
Michael Majerczyk, Jack Morato, John Persinger,
Chris Schloemer, Susanne Watts

Webmaster

Jona Lunde

Academic Advisors

Emily Herff, Dr. Robert Smith, Jennifer Thompson

Contents

Letter from the Editor

Michael Majerczyk

Hi everyone. The cold winter months keep many people indoors and inactive but there is little evidence of the wintertime blues at the Saber and Scroll Journal because the winter months consistently produce interesting and well-researched articles and book reviews. This issue contains works that center on tragedy and heroism. In *The Hundred Years' War: A different Contextual Overview*, Dr. Robert Smith discusses the impact that conflict made on the West and the role that Joan of Arc for played for France in the context of this lengthy conflict. In *The Maiden of France: A Brief Overview of Joan of Arc and the Siege of Orléans*, Cam Rea discusses the life of Joan of Arc. It is clear that she was legendary in her time. Joan's story continues to influence us moderns through art, literature, popular culture, and imagination. Anne Midgely discusses this element of her story in her article, *Joan of Arc through the Ages: In Art and Imagination*.

The Civil War is always a popular topic amongst Saber and Scroll members and this issue includes two articles related to it. Lew Taylor discusses the Battle of New Market and provides a biography of each of the fallen cadets in *"Died on the Field of Honor, Sir." Virginia Military Institute in the American Civil War and the Cadets Who Died at the Battle of New Market: May 15, 1864.* Greg Drummond's article, *Across the Etowah and into the Hell-Hole: Johnston's Lost chance for Victory* in the Atlanta Campaign analyzes the challenges General Joseph Johnston faced.

Member's interest in naval warfare during World War Two continues. Jeff Ballard's *Cape Esperance: The Misunderstood Victory of Admiral Norman Scott* provides a fine narrative of the Battle of Cape Esperance and an in-depth analysis of the tactics employed. Indeed, the emphasis on naval warfare over the last two issues prompted my review of the Air Zoo Aviation Museum.

Book reviews often provide researchers with the current trends in the historiography of a particular topic. If you are interested in the American West, Stan Prager provides a book review of Paul Andrew Hutton's *The Apache Wars: the Hunt for Geronimo, the Apache Kid, and the Captive Boy Who Started the Longest War in American History.*

The Hundred Years' War: A Different Contextual Overview

Dr. Robert G. Smith

The origin of most wars is invariably traceable in a linear sense to certain events or key personalities. World War One is easy—the assassination of the Archduke Franz Ferdinand in Sarajevo gave the Austro-Hungarian Empire its *raison d'*être to deal with its Serbian Problem. World War Two is traceable through a series of events such as the Italian Invasion of Ethiopia, the Marco Polo Bridge Incident in 1937, and perhaps even Munich. In the late twentieth century, Saddam Hussein's invasion of Kuwait was the pretext for the First Gulf War. But the casual student of history would see no obvious historical markers to direct their attention to the immediate causes of the Hundred Years' War.

Here the historian has to conduct a forensic examination of both the economics of feudal Europe and of states and principalities that no longer exist. In the early fourteenth century, Flanders was the industrial heart of Europe, based in large part upon its manufacture of cloth. To meet the demands for its products, the manufacturers of Flanders had to import English fleece. The English Crown in turn became dependent upon this source of foreign revenue. This set poorly with the French, for in the not too distant past the nobility of Flanders had been vassals to the French King. Much like Vladimir Putin's machinations in the Ukraine, the French worked to undermine the English position, supporting the landed nobility in their efforts to rein in the manufactures—those with no nobility whose economic engine was loosening the feudal ties the landed nobility depended upon for their economic well-being. A civil war caused by two different economic systems, manufacturing versus the feudal land system, soon engulfed Flanders. Here is the center of gravity for understanding the Hundred Years' War.[1] Although England's King Henry III relinquished his control of the French territories in 1259, there were still English settlers there. Dealing with them was a source of friction between France and England, giving England an excuse for intervention, much as the Tsar and Soviets used for the pretext of invasions to protect ethnic Russians elsewhere.

The Struggle for Control of France

Ironically, when the editors of the *Saber and Scroll Journal* commissioned an article on the Hundred Years' War, this author accepted the project unenthusiastically. However, as research progressed, the outlines of pre-

Westphalia Europe began to take shape, almost like the movement of tectonic plates reshaping the landmass and political structure of Europe. The aftermath of the Hundred Years' War served to consolidate the power of the French monarchy, which heretofore the claim of the English Crown had usurped from the Crown of France. This consolidation had second and third order effects that are easy to overlook. For France, it meant that it became a dominant continental land power. Moreover, the French began to establish an actual navy. For the English, with the loss of France, their eyes turned elsewhere. Without the loss of France, and the French consolidation, would the Age of Exploration have happened the way that it did? For with the loss of France, the English Crown needed to replace the loss of its French holdings and the associated revenue stream. Hence, by the late sixteenth century following the defeat of the Spanish Armada, both England and France began eyeing the New World discovered by Spain to stake a claim. Perhaps this is the greatest impact of the Hundred Years' War, that with the establishment of France, the preconditions for the Age of Exploration were set.

The Battlefield of the Hundred Years' War

"Pride goeth before the fall" could easily be the epithet for French tactical thinking at Agincourt. But the same epithet fits for Poitiers and Crecy, though by Agincourt the French should have learned from their previous defeats. As an aside, none of the Union Army officers from West Point that fought at the Battle of Fredericksburg in December 1862 must have studied Poitiers. Had they done so, they would have blanched at assaulting such a steep hill against far greater lethality than that projected by the English longbow archers. Most battles were sieges, fought by certain and set rules of war. Raids were utilized to extract political concessions when the English would pillage the countryside, demonstrating to the population that the King of France was powerless to protect them from the depredations of the English.

Artillery was first and foremost the biggest technological advancement of the period. Town walls could no longer withstand the new power of artillery. In turn, this meant one could no longer defend passively and hope the enemy's siege would fail or sickness would ruin their army. By the Battle of Poitiers in 1356, the advent of plated armor lessened the power of the longbow. However, it made walking difficult and running impossible. When dismounted, a French heavy cavalry soldier would soon be exhausted. For when a heavy French cavalryman fell at Poitiers or Agincourt, he could not rise again without assistance. By contrast, the English light infantryman had a steel cap and a breastplate that provided protection to his torso and enabled easy movement.[2]

In terms of command and control, a changing battlefield emerged. This change originated with dominance on the battlefield shifting from shock to missile power. It enabled England's King Edward III and the Black Prince, respectively at Crecy and Poitiers, to establish themselves on high ground and fight the battle as they saw it from that vantage. The change from shock to missile meant that battles became of longer duration and subject to greater control in terms of engaging and for purposes of disengagement.[3]

The most important advance of the period was Henry V's introduction of the Royal Navy. He realized that not having a standing fleet at the ready was an impediment to quick and decisive action. His establishment of a standing fleet gave the English greater maneuverability, as the English armies in France were always dependent upon sea power for supply and reinforcement.

Analysis of the Battle of Agincourt presents a different challenge. Numbers do not match up in various accounts of the battle. In *Cursed Kings,* Jonathan Sumption puts the odds at roughly two to one, which seems baffling.[4] In *The Agincourt War,* Arthur Burne reaches a figure of six thousand English to twenty-five thousand French.[5] The English figures are of course always subject to desertion, straggling, and wastage. Burne also notes that a French historian in recent years, Fenrindad Lot, as well as the German historian Hans Delbrück, reached the astounding conclusion the English outnumbered the French that day. One can at least charitably excuse the

Figure 1. King Henry V, by unknown artist. Oil on panel, late sixteenth or early seventeenth century. National Portrait Gallery, UK.

French historian save for the fact that he panders the same excuse for Crecy.[6] Under the biography of Henry V, *The Harpers Encyclopedia of Military Biography* comes up with a figure of six thousand English to as many as thirty-five thousand French.[7] The battle figures remind one of the Battle of Kursk, where the number of tanks has been massaged by both sides. What is hard to understand is why the French did not allow Henry to simply limp to the coast, dogging his retreat every step of the way. Sumption's opinion probably reflects the prevailing French sentiment that, "Politically it was probably unthinkable, after Henry V's capture of Harfleur and his ostentatious challenges, to let him escape with impunity."[8]

Joan of Arc is harder to assess in the military sense. Nevertheless, in the political and psychological sense, she revitalized the French fighting spirit, acting as a morale force multiplier. It is hard to understand how this peasant girl, albeit from prosperous peasants, was given such an opportunity except to consider that the fortunes of France were at their lowest nadir. Even with Henry V's death in 1422, the French forces were demoralized, and their leadership decimated to the point of conceding defeat to the invading English forces and their allies from Burgundy. If the English took the city of Orleans, it seemed as if French resistance would simply crumble. The French loss at the Battle of the Herrings—where they failed to capture a English resupply train (of herring no less!)—meant the impending loss of Orleans was seemingly the last psychological straw. Instead, Joan led the French to victory at Orleans. More importantly, Joan of Arc changed the rules of the game. No longer was this to be the gentlemanly and leisurely style of warfare. If anything, Joan ushered in an early era of something akin to a predecessor to Total Warfare. In a sense, Machiavelli had been the theorist for what seems to us a period of unregulated warfare, whose influence now began to wane.[9] Joan seemed to have fought with the Augustinian concept of a Just War, an alien concept. Here was now a war not just for some prince or king but a war for the general welfare of the French people, an ideal of all equal before God, and by inference a war on feudalism itself, where the ancient order produced the evil of man subjugating man. Joan changed the French Army's thought to one where it mattered how "it [felt] about the soil and about the people from which it springs."[10] It is small wonder that once Joan had recovered the political and military situation, the French were perhaps not unhappy to abandon her to her fate, as her ideas were revolutionary and a threat to the existing order.

But the French were learning. Like the English, they began setting the foundation for a more professional army, for imitation is the highest form of flattery. There would be no more of the emotional charges like at Poiters or Agincourt that decimated the French forces. The return of the Province of Maine to

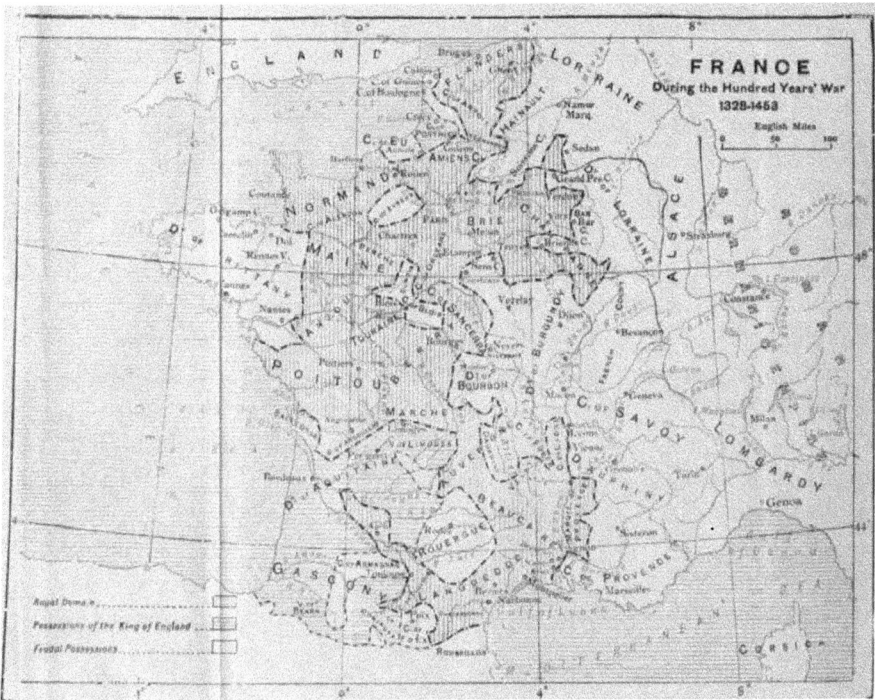

Figure 2. A. Mary F. Robinson, *A short history of France from Caesar's invasion to the Battle of Waterloo*, 1918. Internet Archive Book Images

the French signalled that they had the measure of Henry VI, in whose veins they ascertained did not run the blood of The Black Prince or that of his father, Henry V. Nor when the French began preparations for the invasion of Normandy was anything done by Henry VI, for politics at the court of England were now taking precedence over the defense of the English dominions of France. A small army was hastily assembled and sent over under the command of Sir Thomas Kyriell in 1450. On the way to battle at Formigny, the city folk of Carentan engaged the English rearguard in waist deep water and the French assailed the English with an almost rudimentary form of partisan warfare.[11] Such a brazen action alone speaks volumes of the decline of English influence and the rise of perhaps a French consciousness. Kyriell seemingly had the battle won when another French column showed up, and in contrast to times past where the French showed unwillingness to give battle, charged. The English army died to nearly the last man. And, with

11

the destruction of this English Army, Normandy was lost.

The Political Struggle

Of course, family ties and the lack of an heir often were cause for political turmoil. The quest for a male heir to secure the line was often an obsession for rulers. It is not surprising that this too was one of the underlying political reasons for the Hundred Years' War. Charles IV died heirless in 1328. England's Edward III asserted that the throne of France was his due to his birthright from his mother. Instead, the French nobility crowned Philip VI of Valois. Adding insult to injury, this French usurper attacked the British wine country of Aquitaine, a large province in southwestern France. By feudal law, Aquitaine was a fiefdom to the English Crown. With Philip's attack on Aquitaine and claiming it as rightfully his, war was inevitable. Edward, of course, responded militarily and thus began a long drought of French success on the battlefield through seemingly the rest of the fourteenth century.

If the French military, logistical, and economic structures and population were not already stressed enough by the early fifteenth century, the assassination of the Duke of Orleans led to civil war in France. Much as America's Civil War allowed Napoleon III to crown Maximillian as the Emperor of Mexico, the English—who were seriously threatened with the loss of their Brittany possession—now got a breathing spell. With the soon to be crowned Henry V, this breathing spell saw France soon courting disaster. Yet the English were slow to capitalize upon this opportunity. The always unsettled Scottish border, with the Scots supplied and egged on by France, the faux Richard II paraded about, and then a full blown rebellion in Wales were more than merely distracting to Henry IV, and upon his death Henry V.

The setting as well has many interesting current and near past history parallels. The use of the "assigned" companies who periodically pillaged the French countryside could be thought of as warring by proxies. The Cold War saw many conflicts waged by proxies to not only win control of land but to also sway the court of public opinion at home and in their own regional and global sphere. Both sides used the most important two social media of their day—public letters read as pronouncements in towns and the Catholic Church. The importance of the Catholic Church lay in the fact that the Pope could consecrate one side as the defender of the faith. In addition, at the parish level, the church from the pulpit could sway opinion by preaching for the cause of either the French or English.

Other competing elements affected the West for the next five hundred plus years. Although monarchs ruled both systems, like most of Europe, the two systems of monarchy and government were already heading in different directions. By the end of the Hundred Years' War with the French victorious, France moved to a system of absolute monarchy. The English already had a different approach prior to the war with Magna Carta. However, Henry IV's regicide had different repercussions. For the French, it meant the English were in sense barbarians with a usurper who committed regicide, a crime against God. However, Henry's act served notice that this was an acceptable way to replace the English monarch, and gave the French Crown reason to be nervous about an ambitious French knight. Repercussions of Henry IV's act of seizing the crown by the death of Richard II would help fuel the War of the Roses. Not only did Henry IV have to fear for his crown, but before Henry V's 1415 campaign, a cabal of English nobles under French pay plotted to assassinate Henry the V.

With the disastrous diplomatic decisions of Henry VI, the English Crown lost its remaining lands in 1451. The subsequent loss of a revenue stream to the crown and to the lords who had lost their estates in France, as well as rising unemployment among the professional military class, built resentment. It is easy to see the nexus that if one king could be replaced, then another could as well. In the present day, the horrible decision of Paul Bremer to disband the Iraqi Army in 2003 helped spin Iraq into civil war, much like England post-1451. However, never was the Hundred Years' War like the line from *Mrs. Miniver* "a war of the people."[12] This war was strictly power politics between the Crowns of France and England.

The Sins of Their Fathers - the long-term aspects of The Hundred Years' War

The Hundred Years' War ensured long-term enmity between France and England. The two kingdoms fought a series of proxy frontier wars in the American colonies until Colonel George Washington attacked a French scouting party in Western Pennsylvania, which ignited the French and Indian War in America, or the Seven Years' War in Europe. This war spanned the globe from Canada to Europe and India. Later, Britain often served as the driving force against Napoleon in the various anti-French coalitions. Even in the immediate period before World War One, these two powers nearly came to blows over the Fasho Crisis in 1898. In the mad scramble for colonies, a French expedition to Fashoda tried to seize control of the upper Nile, which would have rendered Britain's position in the Sudan meaningless. In the opening phases of World War One in France, the French were certain that after the initial defeat of the British Expeditionary Force in August

1914 at Mons, the British would make a two hundred plus mile retreat under their commander Field Marshall Sir John French to the sea. Historically, from the Hundred Years' War onward, the British Army used the Royal Navy as an escape valve. The climax of the hatred sowed during the Hundred Years' War came with **Operation Catapult,** the Battle of *Mers-el-Kébir.* On 3 July 1940, the Royal Navy bombarded the French Fleet at its Algerian base of Mers El Kébir. This action by Prime Minister Winston Churchill against his former ally of less than a month before caused the death of the hundreds of French sailors and cemented the French view of Perfidious Albion. Even with the recent Brexit vote by the British, it is possible to see traces of this still simmering dislike of the British for continental entanglements.

Ultimately, it is difficult to conceive that the Hundred Years' War could have ended with any different result other than England's expulsion from France. Much like the Third Reich's gamble to conquer Europe, England—like the Third Reich—was simply over taxed in terms of its resources. It lacked the manpower to hold France, as the available manpower in England simply was not enough to conquer and hold the domain of France. Unlike the later British Empire, the English did not have a technological prowess that gave them a force multiplier. No, the sides were equal in the technology of arms. With the early death of Henry V, England lost its best and perhaps only opportunity to bend France to its knee. Henry died of dysentery a month before Charles VII died, meaning that Henry would have succeeded to the throne of both England and France, a consequence of the earlier Peace Treaty of Troyes. It would be interesting to speculate what could have happened had Henry not died and instead had twenty strong years as regent of both France and England. However, his death coupled with the rise of the Maid of Orleans—who in her short lifetime gave France a holy mission—brought forth a new France, a France for the French. Vercingetorix's dream of a united Gaul may have died at Alesia, but from Orleans arose a new France and its monarchy began to move out of the Feudal Period.

Conclusion

Much like the Third Reich, England won all the famed battles. It was like the heady days of 1941-1942 for the German *Heer* in Russia—crushing all in its path. Agincourt, Crecy, Poitiers . . . yet like the Heer, the English were vanquished. The world of the English in France fell. In its loss of World War One, Imperial Germany focused on the reason for its loss both externally and internally. Never beaten on the battlefield, Germany propagated the myth that it was defeated due to the stab in the back, wielded by leftists and Jews, who poisoned the German body politic with bacillus from abroad. The English, instead, did their version of the piece of American political theater "Who lost China"? that poisoned American politics in the 1950's—as if China was America's to lose. However, France, or at least the parts of France that were for the English Crown to lose, was lost. Losing the territories was bad enough, but with the ill-conceived political decisions of Henry VI, the French witnessed English appeasement like that of Neville Chamberlain in a latter age. That show of weakness, and in French eyes lack of resolution, gave them a window of opportunity to reconquer Normandy and all the other English-held lands. From this arose the antecedents of the War of the Roses, the dynastic struggles Henry VI unleashed by his perceived lack of legitimacy and loss of the English holdings in France.

Notes

1. Lynn Harry Nelson, "The Hundred Years' War, 1336-1453," *Lectures in Medieval History*, University of Kansas, accessed February 27, 2017, http://vlib.us/medieval/lectures/ hundred_years_war.html.

2. Archer Jones, *The Art of War in the Western World* (New York: Oxford University Press, 1987), 165-171.

3. Martin V. Cevald, *Command in War* (Cambridge: Harvard University Press, 1985), 51.

4. Jonathan Sumption, *Cursed Kings: The Hundred Years War IV* (London: Faber & Faber, 2015), 451.

5. Arthur H. Burne, *The Agincourt War* (Hertfordshire, England: Wordsworth Editions, 1999), 90-91.

6. Ibid., 91.

7. Trevor N. Dupuy, Curt Johnson, and David L. Bongard, *The Harpers Encyclopedia of Military Biography* (New York: Castle Books 1995), np.

8. Sumption, 452.

9. Peter Paret, ed., *Makers of Modern Strategy from Machiavelli to the Nuclear Age* (Princeton: Princeton University Press, 1986), 72.

10. S.L.A. Marshall, *Men Against Fire: The Problem of Battle Command in Future War* (New York: William Morrow, 1947), 158.

11. Burne, *The Agincourt War*, 315.

12. *Mrs. Miniver*, directed by William Wyler (Metro-Goldwyn-Mayer, 1942).

Bibliography

Allmand, Christopher. *The Hundred Years War: France and England at War c. 1300-1450*. New York: Cambridge University Press, 1987.

Burne, Lt Col. Alfred H. *The Agincourt War: A Military History of the Hundred Years War from 1369 to 1453*. London: Frontline Books, 1991.

Crevald, Martin V. *Command in War*. Cambridge: Harvard University Press, 1985.

Dupuy, Trevor; Curt Johnson & David L. Bongard. *The Harper Encyclopedia of Military Biography*. New York: Castle Books 1995.

Green, David. *The Hundred Years War: A People's History*. New Haven: Yale University Press, 2014.

Jones, Archer. *The Art of War in the Western World*. New York: Oxford University Press, 1987.

Marshall, S.L.A. *Men Against Fire: The Problem of Battle Command in Future War*. New York: William Morrow, 1947.

Nelson, Dr. Harry L. *The Hundred Years' War, 1336-1453. Lecture University of Kan*sas, http://www.vlib.us/medieval/lectures/hundred_years_war.html

Paret, Peter. *Makers of Modern Strategy from Machiavelli to the Nuclear Age*. Princeton: Princeton University Press, 1986.

Sumption, Jonathan. *Cursed Kings: The Hundred Years War IV*. London: Faber & Faber, 2015.

The Maiden of France: A Brief Overview of Joan of Arc and the Siege of Orléans

Cam Rea

France, embroiled in a war with England in a struggle over the French throne during the Hundred Years' War, would find a savior who in turn was a heretic to the English. This sinner and saint was a woman by the name of Joan of Arc. While most people know that the English burned her at the stake at Vieux Marché in Rouen, most have forgotten her military adventures against the English.

The Peasant Girl

In 1412, Joan of Arc (or Jeanne d'Arc) was born in the village of Domremy located in the Duchy of Bar, France. She was the daughter of poor farmers by the names of Jacques d' Arc and his wife Isabelle. Like the upbringing on any farm, Joan learned primarily agricultural skills. She was said to have been a hardworking and religious child.

Joan's fame came when she claimed to hear the voice of God, which instructed her to expel the English and to have the Dauphin, Charles Valois (Crown Prince of France) crowned king of France. Incredibly, Joan would get her chance to meet with the Dauphin Charles VII when the situation changed for the worse in 1429. In 1429, the city of Orléans, loyal to the French crown, had been under siege by the English for over a year. With

Figure 1. *Jeanne d'Arc*, by Eugène Thirion (1876). The portrait depicts Joan of Arc's awe upon receiving a vision from the Archangel Michael.

Orléans under heavy attack, the uncle of Henry VI, John, Duke of Bedford and the English regent, advanced with a force towards the Duchy of Bar, which at that time was under the rule of Rene, the brother-in-law of Charles Valois.

Divine Revelation

As the English advance seemed unstoppable, the young Joan in the village of Domremy approached the garrison commander, Robert de Baudricourt, and informed him that voices told her to rescue Orléans. She demanded that he assemble some men, provide some resources, and take her to meet with the Dauphin at Chinon. The garrison commander scoffed at the idea of a peasant girl standing before the French Royal Court and sent her away. Not dissuaded, she petitioned Baudricourt's soldiers, and making accurate predictions about the outcomes of battles (apparently proving divine revelation), won the right to appear to the Royal Court.

Joan arrived at Chinon on 23 February 1429. Right before Joan arrived, Charles is said to have disguised himself to see if she would be able to identify

Figure 2. The Siege of Orléans, c. 1493.

him, and to test her "powers" as a prophetess, but it was to no avail, because she bowed before him, and said, "God give you a happy life, sweet King!"[1]

Figure 3. Miniature from *Vigiles du roi Charles VII*. Joan of Arc and Charles VII, king of France.

After a lengthy examination by the theologians, she was found not to be a heretic or insane. With no mental issues found, they advised Charles to let her do what the divine will had apparently commanded her to do. Charles agreed. Before setting off to fight the English, Joan wrote a letter to the English king and English Regent of France:

JESUS, MARY

King of England, render account to the King of Heaven of your royal blood. Return the keys of all the good cities which you have seized, to the Maid. She is sent by God to reclaim the royal blood, and is fully prepared to make peace, if you will give her satisfaction; that is, you must render justice, and pay back all that you have taken.

King of England, if you do not do these things, I am the commander of the military; and in whatever place I shall find your men in France, I will make them flee the country, whether they wish to or not; and if they will not obey, the Maid will have them all killed. She comes sent by the King of Heaven, body for body, to take you out of France, and the Maid promises and certifies to you that if you do not leave France she and her troops will raise a mighty outcry as has not been heard in France in a thousand years. And believe that the King of Heaven has sent her so much power that you will not be able to harm her or her brave army.

To you, archers, noble companions in arms, and all people who are before Orléans, I say to you in God's name, go home to your own country; if you do not do so, beware of the Maid, and of the damages you will suffer. Do not attempt to remain, for you have no rights in France from God, the King of Heaven, and the Son of the Virgin Mary. It is Charles, the rightful heir, to whom God has given France, who will shortly enter Paris in a grand company. If you do not believe the news written of God and the Maid, then in whatever place we may find you, we will soon see who has the better right, God or you.

William de la Pole, Count of Suffolk, Sir John Talbot, and Thomas, Lord Scales, lieutenants of the Duke of Bedford, who calls himself regent of the King of France for the King of England, make a response, if you wish to make peace over the city of Orléans! If you do not do so, you will always recall the damages which will attend you.

Duke of Bedford, who call yourself regent of France for the King of England, the Maid asks you not to make her destroy you. If you do not render her satisfaction, she and the French will perform the greatest feat ever done in the name of Christianity.

Done on the Tuesday of Holy Week (March 22, 1429). HEAR
THE WORDS OF GOD AND THE MAID.[2]

One can definitely suspect that the king of England and the English Regent of France did not take it to be cordial.

Figure 4. Joan of Arc depicted on horseback, illustration
from a 1505 manuscript.

Religious War

Joan of Arc, as a symbol of God's will to the French, had turned a generational Anglo-French battle over thrones into a religious war.

Joan convinced the leading French theologians and France's future king that the Divine had sent her; they in turn, provided her with armor to wear and placed a force of four thousand men under her command. She set off towards Orléans soon after, carrying a white banner depicting Jesus, the Virgin Mary, and two angels.

On 29 April 1429, she entered Orléans. There she met with the commander of the garrison, John, comte de Dunois, the Bastard of Orléans. Upon meeting him, she demanded that he immediately attack the English. However, Dunois was not ready. While he was preparing with the now additional four thousand troops who accompanied Joan, Joan decided to approach and shout at the English troops. She informed them that she was the one sent by God—the "maiden"—and said to them "Begone, or I will make you go" but the English upon hearing her message, hurled insults back.[3] On 30 April, the Orléans militia, under the command of Étienne de Vignoles, assaulted the English at the Boulevard of Saint-Pouair, but the attack proved unsuccessful. Joan called out to Sir William Glasdale at Les Tourelles stating, "Yield to God's command."[4] The English replied by calling her a "cowgirl."[5] They made it known to Joan that if they captured her they would surely burn her. But even in their anger, they were also cautious.

On 1 May, Dunois and a small band of men, along with Joan and some soldiers, left to bring the army back to Blois. During this small mission, the English did not attempt to engage the French even though they knew she was among this small army. Interestingly, the reason for not engaging the French seems to have been due to fear, for the lower English ranks feared that she had some supernatural powers and to risk taking her dead or alive was detrimental to their own wellbeing. On 3 May, the main body of Joan's relief force arrived. She made it clear to the French soldiers and officers that God had sent her, as she rode in at the head as a priest and chanted from the book of Psalms.

With Joan and four thousand men in Orléans, the Armagnacs—prominent Orleanists in French politics—attacked the outlying English fort of Saint Loup on 4 May and captured it. Feeling confident after the capture of Saint Loup, the French were preparing to attack the weakest English bastions on the south bank of the Loire the next day. However, despite the win, Joan decided on a temporary one-day truce to honor the Feast of the Ascension on 5 May. It was during this truce that Joan wrote a letter for the English stating, "You, men of England, who have no right to this Kingdom of France, the king of Heaven orders and notifies you

Figure 5. *Joan of Arc*, oil on parchment, c. 1450-1500.
Miniature portrait in an illustrated manuscript. Centre
Historique des Archives Nationales, Paris, France.

through me, Joan the Maiden, to leave your fortresses and go back to your own country; or I will produce a clash of arms to be eternally remembered. And this is the third and last time I have written to you; I shall not write anything further."[6] She gave this letter to a crossbowman and he shot the letter into the English fortress of Les Tourelles. In the fortress, an archer retrieved the message and said, "Read, here is the news!" The English commander replied, "Here is news from the Armagnac whore!"[7] Joan is said to have wept after hearing their reply.

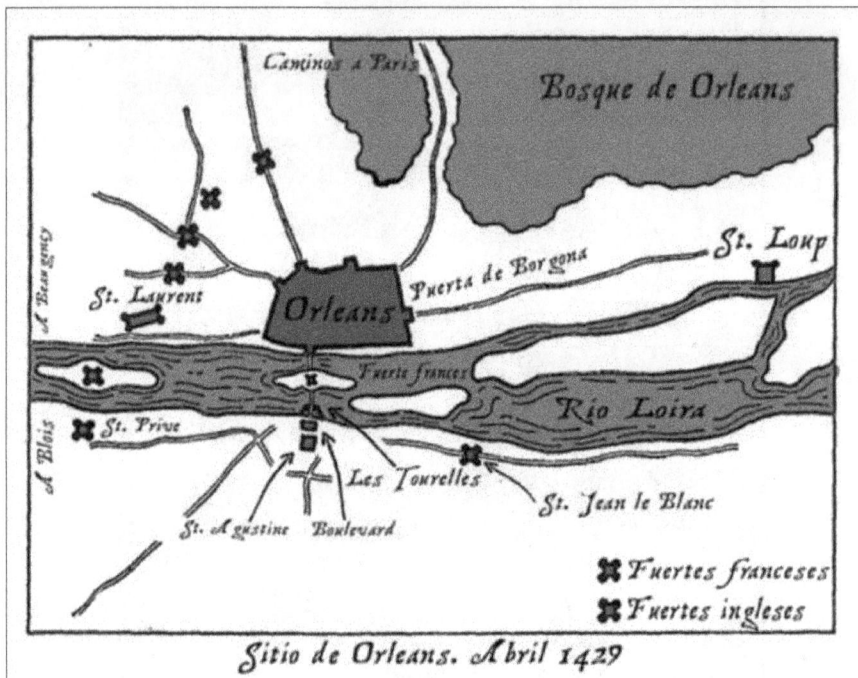

Figure 6. Fortifications around Orléans at the time of the siege. English forts are depicted in red, French forts are depicted in blue. Map by Milo Tatch, published under GNU Free Documentation License.

The English Downfall

On 6 May, the French set off and reached Fort Saint-Jean-le-Blanc. However, they found it empty. The Armagnacs continued to advance. The English appeared outside the fort and attempted a cavalry charge but were defeated and driven back into their stronghold.

With the English bottled up, the Armagnacs continued on, capturing another English fort near the Les Augustins monastery. From here, the Armagnacs held steady on the south bank of the river Loire before engaging the English fortress of Les Tourelles the following morning on 7 May.

While Joan partook in many of the battles, she did so from a support role, encouraging the men, boosting morale and confidence, and she also helped many of the wounded before she was herself wounded above the breast by an arrow at Les Tourelles. She is said to have pulled the arrow out with her own hand and dressed the wound with oil. After treating her wound and getting some rest, she noticed French troops retreating from the fortress. She quickly grabbed her standard, and stormed towards the fortress. She stuck her banner into the ground and shouted encouragement to the men to fight on.

Sir William Glasdale and his small English force, seeing that they could

Figure 7. France in the Hundred Years' War, by Aliesin. Published under GNU Free Documentation License.

hold no longer in their earth-and-timber fortress, and after witnessing that Joan was not dead, fled the flimsy ill-constructed fort for the safer stone fortress of Les Tourelles. It was at this moment that Joan saw Glasdale fleeing and shouted to him. "Glasdale! Glasdale! Yield to the King of Heaven! You called me a whore, but I have great pity on your soul and the souls of your men!"[8] Whether Glasdale stopped or not is up for debate, but during the chaos around them, a French incendiary boat became wedged beneath the wooden drawbridge, causing it to catch fire. Glasdale and his men attempting to cross it to reach the safety of Les Tourelles, did not make it, for the bridge caught fire and soon weakened. The bridge could not hold the weight of the men and it disintegrated and gave way. Glasdale, and the men with him, crashed into the river and drowned due to the weight of their armor.

Figure 8. French troops of Joan of Arc besieging the English fortifications during the siege of Orléans, c. fifteenth century.

Tables Turned

The seemingly unstoppable French advance caused the English to surrender the fortress, which resulted in a French victory that lifted the siege of Orléans. Nine days after Joan's arrival at Orléans, the siege had collapsed. This military victory was a major turning point in the Hundred Years' War. Afterwards, more fortresses fell within the duchy, causing the English to send forces to stop the advancement but they were in turn defeated. In just a few weeks, the English from the Loire valley were swept aside and Bedford, the English Regent of France, had lost much of his supplies, which greatly crippled any further English advance for the time being.

Figure 9. *Joanne of Arc Falls Prisoner at Compiègne*, by Jules Eugene Lenepveu, c. 1886-1890.

Joan partook in many successful military operations until the English eventually captured her. Joan of Arc and the French army marched toward the defense of Compiègne against the Burgundian army, led by John of Luxembourg, and arrived on 14 May 1430. However, on 22 May, Joan went out during a sortie and surprised the Burgundians. While Joan's attack was effective, the Burgundian forces refused defeat, rallied their forces, and defeated her men. Joan retreated toward the gates and continued to fight, as she refused to admit defeat. This stubborn will allowed her to fall into the hands of her enemy, for the commander of the town left the gates open long enough for Joan and her forces to enter. However, seeing Joan refusing to disengage and the enemy ever so close to the entrance, the commander ordered the gate shut, sealing Joan's fate.

After the Burgundians captured her, they imprisoned Joan at Beaulieu Castle at Rouen. After a lengthy imprisonment and trial, the English executed the Maiden of France on 30 May 1431.

The author previously published a slightly different version of this article on his blog at http://www.camrea.org/.

Notes

1. Régine Pernoud, Marie-Véronique Clin, *Joan of Arc: Her Story,* trans. Jeremy duQuesnay Adams, ed. Bonnie Wheeler, (New York: St. Martin's Press, 1999), 103-137, 209.

2. Joan of Arc, Letter to the King of England, 1429, trans. Belle Tuten from M. Vallet de Vireville, ed. *Chronique de la Pucelle, ou Chronique de Cousinot* (Paris: Adolphe Delahaye, 1859), 281-283, https://legacy.fordham.edu/halsall/source/joanofarc.asp.

3. Joan of Arc, quoted in Wm. E. Baumgaertner, "1429-The Maid of Orléans," *A Timeline of Fifteenth Century England 1398-1509* (Victoria, BC: Trafford Publishing, 2009).

4. Joan M. Edmunds, *The Mission of Joan of Arc* (Forest Row, East Essex: Temple Lodge Publishing, 2008), 46.

5. Ibid.

6. Joan of Arc, Third Letter to the English at Orléans May 5, 1429, accessed January 15, 2017, https://archive.joan-of-arc.org/joanofarc_letter_May_5_1429.html.

7. Allen Williamson, "Segment 6: Orléans, Part II," Joan of Arc Biography, accessed January 15, 2017, http://www.joan-of-arc.org/joanofarc_life_summary_orleans2.html.

8. Ibid.

Bibliography

Baumgaertner, Wm. E. *A Timeline of Fifteenth Century England - 1398 to 1509*. Victoria, B.C., Canada: Trafford Publishing, 2009.

Bradbury, Jim. *The Routledge Companion to Medieval Warfare*. London: Routledge, 2004.

Edmunds, Joan M. *The Mission of Joan of Arc*. Forest Row, East Essex: Temple Lodge Publishing, 2008.

DeVries, Kelly. *Joan of Arc: A Military Leader*. Stroud: Sutton Publishing, Ltd., 1999.

Dupuy, Trevor N., Curt Johnson, and David L. Bongard. *The Harper Encyclopedia of Military Biography*. New York, NY: HarperCollins, 1992.

Joan of Arc. Letter to the King of England, 1429. Translated by Belle Tuten from M. Vallet de Vireville, ed. *Chronique de la Pucelle, ou Chronique de Cousinot*. Paris: Adolphe Delahaye, 1859, 281-283. https://legacy.fordham.edu/halsall/source/joanofarc.asp

_____. Third Letter to the English at Orléans. May 5, 1429. Accessed January 17, 2017. https://archive.joan-of-arc.org/joanofarc_letter_May_5_1429.html.

Mirabal, Laura. *Joan of Arc: The Lily of France*. Bloomington, IN: Authorhouse, 2010.

Pernoud, Régine, Marie-Véronique Clin, *Joan of Arc: Her Story*. Translated by Jeremy duQuesnay Adams. Edited by Bonnie Wheeler. New York: St. Martin's Press, 1999.

Richey, Stephen W. *Joan of Arc: The Warrior Saint*. Westport, CT: Praeger, 2003.

Tuckey, Janet. *Joan of Arc, "the Maid."* London: M. Ward & Co, 1880.

Wagner, John A. *Encyclopedia of the Hundred Years War*. Westport, CT: Greenwood Press, 2006.

Williamson, Allen. "Segment 6: Orléans, Part II," *Joan of Arc Biography*. 2014. Accessed January 15, 2017. http://www.joan-of-arc.org/joanofarc_life_summary_orleans2.html.

Joan of Arc through the Ages: In Art and Imagination

Anne Midgley

Since her death at the hands of the English in 1431, Joan of Arc has inspired and puzzled millions. The poor peasant girl who rallied the French to victory at Orléans has fuelled the imagination of artists, authors, poets, and cinematographers. Over the past six centuries, the enigmatic Joan has appealed to not only the people of France, but also to groups as diverse as Philippine and Macedonian revolutionaries, literary societies, American suffragists, and temperance advocates. Yet, according to one Victorian writer, she has also alarmed and troubled many, for according to her assessment, "There is no figure in history more incendiary to the imagination than this Joan of Arc."[1]

From Heretic to Saint: The Trials of St. Joan of Arc

Cam Rea's article "The Maiden of France: A Brief Overview of Joan of Arc and the Siege of Orléans," published in this issue of the *Saber and Scroll Journal*, well details the French military victories that Joan inspired against the English and their French allies, the Burgundians. The English and their allies feared and detested Joan; however, her loyalty to the Dauphin of France, Charles, and her visionary leadership in battle inspired the French Armagnacs to repulse their enemies, lift the siege of Orléans, and win a number of subsequent military victories. These victories eventually led to the coronation of Charles VII as the king of France on 17 July 1429. Out of gratitude, Charles ennobled Joan and her family on 29 December 1429. He provided them with the name of Du Lis and established lilies for their coat of arms. On 24 May 1430, a surprise Burgundian attack on the town of Compiègne led to Joan's capture. She became a prisoner of John of Luxemburg, who sold her to the English. The English desired her death. This prompted the charge of heresy and the infamous ecclesiastical trial that resulted in her death sentence.[2] The court documents record the Sentence of Excommunication against Joan, stating,

> [T]hat you have been on the subject of thy pretended divine revelations and apparitions lying, seducing, pernicious, presumptuous, lightly believing, rash, superstitious, a divineress

and blasphemer towards God and the Saints, a despiser of God Himself in His Sacraments; a prevaricator of the Divine Law, of sacred doctrine and of ecclesiastical sanctions; seditious, cruel, apostate, schismatic, erring on many points of our Faith, and by all these means rashly guilty towards God and Holy Church. And also, because that often, very often, not only by Us on Our part but by Doctors and Masters learned and expert, full of zeal for the salvation of thy soul, you have been duly and sufficiently warned to amend, to correct thyself and to submit to the disposal, decision, and correction of Holy Mother Church, which you have not willed, and have always obstinately refused to do, having even expressly and many times refused to submit thyself to our Lord the Pope and to the General Council; for these causes, as hardened and obstinate in thy crimes, excesses and errors, WE DECLARE THEE OF RIGHT EXCOMMUNICATE AND HERETIC; and after your errors have been destroyed in a public preaching, We declare that you must be abandoned and that We do abandon thee to the secular authority, as a member of Satan, separate from the Church, infected with the leprosy of heresy, in order that you may not corrupt also the other members of Christ; praying this same power, that, as concerns death and the mutilation of the limbs, it may be pleased to moderate its judgment; and if true signs of penitence should appear in thee, that the Sacrament of Penance may be administered to thee.[3]

Despite her excommunication, prior to her execution Joan received the sacraments of Confession and the Holy Eucharist. On 30 May 1431 at Rouen, the English burned Joan at the stake. Not satisfied with her death alone, the executioner had her body burned again. The fire did not consume her heart, which the executioner found intact; however, "for fear lest [her] remains . . . be used for witchcraft . . . [he had it] thrown into the Seine."[4]

In 1450, Charles VII realized that Joan's death as a heretic sullied his own reign, as her heroism had led to his coronation. Accordingly, on 13 February 1450, Charles tasked one of his counsellors, Guillaume Bouillé, "to inquire into the conduct of the Trial undertaken against Jeanne by 'our ancient enemies the English,' who, 'against reason, had cruelly put her to death,' and to report the result of his investigations to the Council."[5] Bouillé's inquiry ended several months later, after relatively few testimonies, in part because the French did not wish to antagonize the English. In 1452, Cardinal Guillaume d'Estouteville re-opened the investigation, but the new round of inquiries also ended without result. Joan's family petitioned the Pope, and in 1455, Pope Calixtus III agreed to the family's request. The Trial of Nullification ended in 1456 with a sentence of rehabilitation—in essence, voiding the conclusions of the original trial. The findings stipulated that the processes and sentences of the previous trial were "full of cozonage, iniquity, inconsequences, and manifest errors, in fact as well as in law; . . . they have boon, are, and shall be-as well as the aforesaid Abjuration, their execution, and all that followed-null, non-existent, without value or effect." Furthermore, the court declared that, "[Joan] and her relatives, Plaintiffs in the actual Process, have not, on account of the said Trial, contracted nor incurred any mark or stigma of infamy; we declare them quit and purged of all the consequences of those same Processes; we declare them, in so far as is necessary, entirely purged thereof by this present."[6]

The nullification trial removed the charges of heresy; it did not establish evidence of holiness, nor consider her death to be that of a martyr. No cult developed to advocate for her sanctity nor were any miracles attributed to Joan until almost five centuries following her death. Yet, Pius II beatified Joan in 1909 and Benedict XV canonized her on 16 May 1920. The reasons for this are worthy of investigation. Church historian Larissa Juliet Taylor claims that complex French and Vatican politics played a role in Joan's canonization, although it did follow proper Church procedures, including the research and testimony of several of the Sacred Congregation's Devil's Advocates. Taylor claims that Joan's cause célèbre lay dormant until the mid-nineteenth century when historians, particularly Jules Michelet and Jules Quicherat began to research Joan, who had become a symbol for both the republican and monarchists of a much-divided France. Taylor notes that Félix Dupanloup, a French scholar and priest, began his role as Bishop of Orléans with "an encomium of Joan that attracted international attention,"[7] as he hoped to return France to its religious roots. Dupanloup became Joan's champion, introducing "the cause for her beatification [to Rome], and [raising] the first funds towards a new monument in her honor."[8]

Devil's Advocate Augustine Caprara contended, "[T]his praise of sanctity has come to her only in our own time,"[9] and that "no miracles or cult was attested."[10] According to Taylor, Pope Pius II "asked the cardinals and consultants of the Sacred Congregation of Rites to pray with him 'in so difficult a manner'."[11] The Pope approved Joan's cause for beatification to proceed on 6 January 1904. Shortly thereafter, the Sacred Congregation approved three miracles that occurred through her intercession, and Pope Pius X declared Joan "Blessed" on 11 April

1909.[12]

World War I devastated Europe between 1914 and 1918. Taylor claims that the relationship between the Vatican and France worsened during that war and that tensions between both parties ran unabated. Yet in 1920, two years after the "War to end all Wars," Pope Benedict XV canonized Joan of Arc, the symbol of France's glory. While Joan's route to sainthood took an arduous journey, and her ultimate elevation to Saint Joan of Arc contained an element of political mediation between France and the Vatican, ultimately, the Church recognized Joan as a member of the heavenly Church Triumphant—a fitting tribute to the Maid of France, the young girl whose military exploits saved France.[13]

Joan of Arc in Art

During a recent lecture at the Farnsworth Art Museum, distinguished professor of medieval French literature, Nadia Margolis, stated that Joan of Arc "has been depicted in more images than anybody else except Jesus Christ."[14] The earliest artistic representation of Joan of Arc is a sketch by Clément de Fauquembergue, dated from 1429 and made during her lifetime, though it is unlikely that the artist saw Joan in person.[15] Kristi L. Castleberry, who created the brochure for the 2009 Rossell Hope Robbins Library exhibit on Joan of Arc, noted that Joan presented artists with "a unique challenge. There was no precedent for representing a woman who dressed as a man but called herself the Maid, no visual model for a peasant girl who rode next to the king to his coronation."[16] She further noted, "Medieval and Early Modern artists used a variety of visual cues to

Figure 1. *Joan of Arc*, sketch by Clément de Fauquembergue, 1429.

signal Joan's identity and [avoided] the troubling fact that Joan's image defied categorical representation."[17]

As noted earlier, once Joan's Trial of Nullification reached a successful completion, interest in her waned until the nineteenth century, at which time she became a favorite subject of painters and illustrators. In "Saint, Soldier, Spirit, Savior: The Images of Joan of Arc," Elizabeth Foxwell noted that between 1850 and 1930, artists created over three hundred fifty representations of Joan's life and exploits, depicting her "as a defender of the monarchy, the epitome of French courage, [the] loyal servant of God, the symbol of a united France, and liberty."[18] Foxwell classified artistic images of Joan in three categories—"in armor, [representing] heroic virtue, at the stake, [depicting her as a] saint, martyr, sacrifice for France, and listening to voices [dramatizing her as a] prophet, spirit, obedient daughter of God."[19] She described in particular detail a mural completed in 1909 by Louis Maurice Boutet de Monvel, *The Vision and the Inspiration*, which includes Joan as well as St. Michael the Archangel, St. Catherine of Alexandria, and St. Margaret. According to Joan, the voices of these three saints counselled and guided her from the age of thirteen until the time of her death.[20]

Figure 2. *The Vision and the Inspiration*, oil and gold leaf on canvas by Louis Maurice Boutet de Monvel, c. 1907-1909, National Gallery of Art.

A similar painting of Joan done by Jules Bastien-LePage in 1879 depicts Joan in her parents' garden with the apparitions of her saints in the background. Artistic representations of Joan have reflected not only her life but also reinterpreted her in a multitude of symbolic and allegorical ways. In some paintings, the artist portrays Joan in a manner reminiscent of the Virgin Mary, while in others she appears as a chaste warrior similar to the goddess Athena.

Interpretations of Joan have varied through time, as well, particularly in response to challenges faced by France. Foxwell notes that during the Bourbon Restoration, artists portrayed Joan as a defender of the monarchy. Representations of Joan were particularly popular amongst the French following their defeat in the Franco-Prussian War.[21]

Images of Joan inspired American suffragists in the early twentieth century. The Paul Dubois equestrian statue of Joan of Arc, dedicated on 6 January 1922 and located in Washington D.C. was a gift from the Society of French Women of New York to the women of the United States. Joan's unique appeal continues to be re-imagined today. "The Maid of France and Popular Culture" section of this paper provides a further analysis of this topic.[22]

Joan of Arc in Literature

Christine de Pizan penned perhaps the earliest writing about Joan, the *Ditié de Jeanne d'Arc* (The Song of Joan of Arc), which she wrote during Joan's lifetime. Christine's poetry speaks to great pride in Joan's military prowess, and hails Joan as the champion of France:

> She frees France from its enemies,
> Recovering citadels and castles.
> No army ever did so much,
> Not even a hundred thousand vassals!
> And of our brave and able folk,
> She is the chief and first commander.
> God makes it so; not even Hector
> Nor Achilles could withstand her.[23]

Shakespeare's Henry VI, Part 1, on the other hand, presents Joan far differently.

> A witch, by fear, not force, like Hannibal,
> Drives back our troops and conquers as she lists:
> So bees with smoke and doves with noisome stench
> Are from their hives and houses driven away.
> They call'd us for our fierceness English dogs;
> Now, like to whelps, we crying run away.[24]

Detailed records from the trials of Joan of Arc provide incredible insight into her life. They have inspired authors from the fifteenth century until the present day. Castleberry claims that Mark Twain's *Personal Recollections of Joan of Arc* published in 1895 is perhaps the "first thoroughly researched version of Joan."[25] Twain held an unapologetically positive vision of Joan, pronouncing in *Personal*

Recollections, "Whatever thing men call great, look for it in Joan of Arc, and there you will find it,"[26] as well as "It took six thousand years to produce her; her like will not be seen in the earth again in fifty thousand."[27] In Twain's "Saint Joan of Arc" published in *Harpers Monthly Magazine,* he described Joan as, "easily and by far the most extraordinary person the human race has ever produced."[28] On the other hand, George Bernard Shaw's play, *Saint Joan* is dramatically different. Written in 1924 shortly after Joan's canonization, Shaw provides extensive historical background in his preface to the play. He cautions his audience to remember that Joan was "only a girl in her teens. . . . She knew nothing of iron hands in velvet gloves: she just used her fists."[29]

It is beyond the scope of this paper to provide a detailed historiography of the academic works on Joan of Arc. Suffice it to say, that the scholarship is extraordinarily extensive, and at times contradictory. Castleberry points to Margolis's *Joan of Arc in History, Literature, and Film: A Select, Annotated Bibliography* as a starting point for interested scholars.[30]

Joan of Arc on the Silver Screen

Though she had been dead for nearly half a millennium, Joan of Arc began her film career in 1916, with Cecil B. DeMille's first historical epic, *Joan the Woman.*[31] Other film representations followed, perhaps the best being Theordor Dreyer's *The Passion of Joan of Arc* (1928), which Roger Ebert reviewed in 1997, stating that "to see [Renee Maria] Falconetti in Dreyer's [film] is to look into eyes that will never leave you."[32] Ebert quoted Pauline Kael, "It may be the finest performance ever recorded on film."[33] According to Ebert, the director, Dreyer, threw out the original screenplay and in its place, used transcripts from Joan's first trial. Ebert sums up the power of Dreyer's version of Joan of Arc:

Figure 3. Poster for *Joan the Woman* by Cecil B. DeMille, starring Geraldine Farrar. 1916.

> To modern audiences, raised on films where emotion is conveyed by dialogue and action more than by

37

faces, a film like "The Passion of Joan of Arc" is an unsettling experience—so intimate we fear we will discover more secrets than we desire. Our sympathy is engaged so powerfully with Joan that Dreyer's visual methods—his angles, his cutting, his closeups—don't play like stylistic choices, but like the fragments of Joan's experience. Exhausted, starving, cold, in constant fear, only 19 when she died, she lives in a nightmare where the faces of her tormentors rise up like spectral demons.[34]

Victor Fleming's 1948 film, *Joan of Arc,* starring Ingrid Bergman, also gained tremendous acclaim. Bosley Crowther, who reviewed the movie for the New York Times claimed that the movie was one of the "most magnificent films ever made;"[35] however, he faulted it for perhaps missing the "mystery, the meaning and magnificence of the poor girl called Joan."[36] Other highly regarded films on Joan's life and death include Otto Preminger's 1957 film *Saint Joan* and Roberto Rossellini's 1954 *Joan of Arc at the Stake* in which Ingrid Bergman again appeared as Joan.[37]

The Maid of France and Popular Culture

Perhaps nowhere is Joan of Arc more continually re-imagined than in popular culture. It is safe to say that Joan of Arc is a cultural phenomenon, a person

Figure 4. *Joan of Arc,* World War I British propaganda.

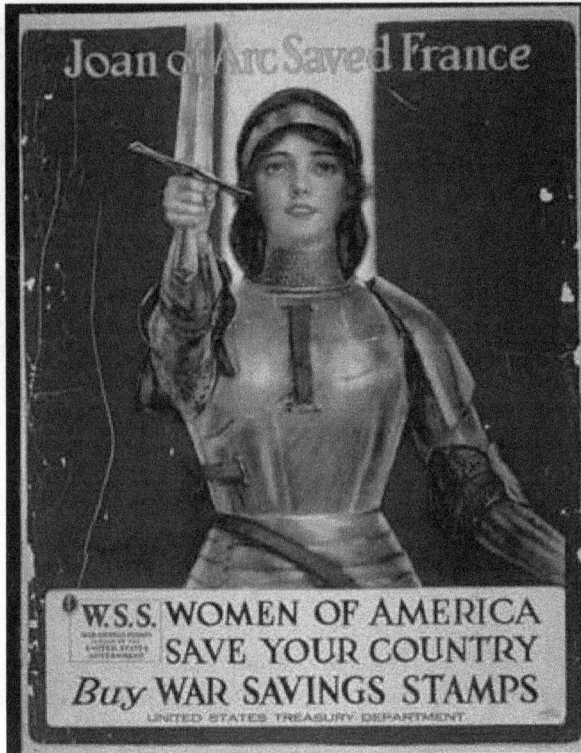

Figure 5. Joan of Arc saved France—Women of
America, save your country—Buy War Savings
Stamps, Library of Congress.

with unique appeal who has fascinated diverse people throughout the last six
centuries. Castleberry's study of Joan in popular culture notes that Joan's image has
been "romanticized, politicized, propagandized, and advertised."[38] Universities
offer classes on Joan of Arc, with titles as strange as "Joan of Arc: History,
Literature, and Film. Superhero, Crazy Trans-Kid, Saint, or Fraud?" to the more
simple "History 401: Joan of Arc."[39]

Both the United States and Britain used Joan's image to sell war bonds
during World War I. Castleberry's "Re-Imaging Joan: Appropriations of Joan of
Arc" catalogues appropriate as well as questionable uses of Joan's image, ranging
from First Communion medals to Joan of Arc Butter Beans.

However, the Thompson Cigar Company has perhaps shown the poorest taste of all commercial appropriations of Joan's image by her to hawk Joan of Arch Robusto Connecticut, a mild cigar.[40]

In perhaps the most recent re-imagination of Joan, the LGBT community has adopted her as an icon.[41] In articles from "Joan of Arc and 9 Other 'Queer' Saints" to books such as *Transgender Warriors: Making History from Joan of Arc to Dennis Rodman,* Joan has gained another loyal following.[42]

Conclusion

Since her life and death in the early fifteenth century, Joan of Arc has defied classification. Her youth, visions, heroism, military accomplishments— even her manner of dressing and trial and death—have made her the subject of countless forms of re-imagination in history, art, literature, film, and popular culture. Perhaps no individual has been analysed and interpreted more than Joan of Arc, yet her unique appeal continues to gain new advocates amongst both religious and secular people. She truly was one-of-a-kind, making it easy for most to agree with Mark Twain that she was "easily and by far the most extraordinary person the human race has ever produced."[43]

Notes

1. James A. Freeman, "Joan of Arc: Soldier, Saint, Symbol—of What," *Journal of Popular Culture* 41, no. 4 (August 2008): 601-634, accessed January 16, 2017, *Academic Search Premier,* EBSCO*host*; Shelley Armitage, review of Visions of the *Maid: Joan of Arc in American Film and Culture* by Robin Blaetz, *Journal of American History* 90, no. 2 (September 2003): 676-677, accessed January 16, 2017, *Academic Search Premier,* EBSCO*host*; Elizabeth Foxwell, "Saint, Soldier, Spirit, Savior: The Images of Joan of Arc," *Minerva* XII, no. 3 (September 30, 1994): 36, accessed January 16, 2017, https://search.proquest.com/docview/222786451?accountid=8289.

2. Herbert Thurston, "St. Joan of Arc," *The Catholic Encyclopedia*, vol. 8 (New York: Robert Appleton Company, 1910, accessed January 17, 2017, http://www.newadvent.org/cathen/08409c.htm; Larissa Juliet Taylor, "Joan of Arc, The Church, and the Papacy, 1429-1920," *The Catholic Historical Review* 98, no. 2 (April 2012): 217-240, accessed January 17, 2017, https://search-proquest-com.ezproxy1.apus.edu/docview/1013675739? accountid= 8289.

3. Mathias Gabel and Carlyn Iuzzolino, trans., "Second Process: The Relapse, Adjudication and Death Sentence," *Saint Joan of Arc's Trial of Condemnation,* 1903, accessed January 17, 2017, http://www.stjoan-center.com/Trials/index.html#nullification.

4. Anatole France, "Chapter XIV, The Trial for Relapse—Second Sentence—Death of the Maid," *The Life of Joan of Arc*, trans., Winifred Stephens (London: John Lane Company, 1908), accessed January 17, 2017, http://www.gutenberg.org/files/19488/19488.txt.

5. Mathias Gabel and Carlyn Iuzzolino, trans., "Introductory Notes to the Nullification Trial," *Saint Joan of Arc's Trial of Nullification,* 1903, accessed January 17, 2017, http://www.stjoan-center.com/Trials/index.html#nullification.

6. Mathias Gabel and Carlyn Iuzzolino, trans., "Concluding Document: Sentence of Rehabilitation," *Saint Joan of Arc's Trial of Nullification*, 1903, accessed January 17, 2017, http:// www.stjoan-center.com/Trials/index.html#nullification.

7. Taylor, "Joan of Arc," The Catholic Historical Review, 238.

8. Joseph Sollier, "Felix-Antoine-Philibert Dupanloup," *The Catholic Encyclopedia* Vol. 5 (New York: Robert Appleton Company, 1909), accessed January 18, 2017, http://www.newadvent.org/cathen/05202a.htm.

9. Taylor, "Joan of Arc," 239.

10. Ibid., 239.

11. Ibid., 240.

12. "The Beautification and Canonization of Saint Joan of Arc," *Joan Directory*, accessed January 18, 2017, http://www.jehannedarc.org/canonization.html.

13. Taylor, "Joan of Arc," The Catholic Historical Review, 240.

14. Nadia Margolis, "Joan of Arc from Medieval Europe to Modern America: A Visual History," (lecture at Farnsworth Art Museum, recorded April 14, 2016), accessed January 18, 2017, https://vimeo.com/163032863.

15. Kristi J. Castleberry, "Joan of Arc's Brief Life and Long Afterlife," River Campus Libraries, University of Rochester, 2009, accessed January 18, 2017, http://www.library.rochester.edu/robbins/joanexhibition.

16. Ibid.

17. Ibid.

18. Ibid.

19. Foxwell, "Saint, Soldier, Spirit, Savior," *Minerva.*

20. "Her Voices," *Portraits of a Saint*, accessed January 18, 2017, http://saint-joan-of-arc.com/voices.htm.

21. Ibid.

22. Ibid.; Joan of Arc, *DC Memorialist,* accessed January 18, 2017, http:// dcmemorialist.com/joan-of-arc/.

23. Christine De Pisan, verse XXXVI, *Ditié de Jeanne d'Arc*, ed. Angus J. Kennedy and Kenneth Varty, trans. L. Shopkow (Oxford: Society for the Study of Medieval Languages and Literature, 1977), accessed January 18, 2017, http://www.indiana.edu/~dmdhist/joan.htm.

24. William Shakespeare, *Henry VI*, Part 1, Act I, Scene V, accessed January 18, 2017, http://shakespeare.mit.edu/1henryvi/full.html.

25. Castleberry, "Joan of Arc's Brief Life and Long Afterlife."

26. Mark Twain, "Joan of Arc," Directory of Mark Twain maxims, quotations, and various opinions, accessed January 18, 2017, http://www.twainquotes.com/JoanofArc.html.

27. Ibid.

28. Ibid.

29. George Bernard Shaw, *Saint Joan: A Chronicle Play in Six Scenes and An Epilogue*, 1924, accessed January 18, 2017, http://gutenberg.net.au/ebooks02/0200811h.html.

30. Castleberry, "Joan of Arc's Brief Life and Long Afterlife."

31. Michael Barson, "Cecil B. DeMille, American Film Director," *Encyclopedia Britannica*, September 4, 2013, accessed January 18, 2017, https://www.britannica.com/biography/Cecil-B-DeMille.

32. Roger Ebert, Review of The Passion of Joan of Arc by Theordor Dreyer, February 16, 1997, accessed January 18, 2017, http://www.rogerebert.com/reviews/great-movie-the-passion-of-joan-of-arc-1928.

33. Ibid.

34. Ibid.

35. Bosley Crowther, "Ingrid Bergman Plays Title Role in 'Joan of Arc' at Victoria," The New York Times, November 12, 1948, accessed January 18, 2017, http://www.nytimes.com/movie/review?res=9403E2D6143DEE3ABC4A52DFB7678383659EDE.

36. Ibid.

37. Foxwell, "Saint, Soldier, Spirit, Savior," *Minerva*.

38. Castleberry, "Joan of Arc's Brief Life and Long Afterlife."

39. Jeremy duQ Adams and Bonnie Wheeler, "Joan of Arc: History, Literature, and Film. Superhero, Crazy Trans-Kid, Saint, of Fraud?" English 3371, History 3357, accessed January 18, 2017, http://www.smu.edu/~/media/Site/mayterm/2015Syllabus/D-1153_ENGL_3371-HIST_3357_AdamsWheelerSyll.ashx?la=en; Ken Pennington, "History 401: Joan of Arc," accessed January 18, 2017, http://classes.maxwell.syr.edu/his401/index.htm.

40. Joan of Arch Robusto Connecticut, Thompson Cigar, accessed January 18, 2017, https://www.thompsoncigar.com/product/JOAN-OF-ARCH-ROBUSTO-CONNECTICUT/94816.uts.

41. Kittredge Cherry, "Joan of Arc: Cross-dressing warrior-saint," *Jesus in Love Blog*, accessed January 18, 2017, http://jesusinlove.blogspot.com/2013/05/joan-of-arc-cross-dressing-warrior-saint.html.

42. Noah Michelson, "Joan of Arc and 9 Other 'Queer' Saints," *The Huffington Post*, December 6, 2011, accessed January 18, 2017, http://www.huffingtonpost.com/2011/12/05/joan-of-arc-and-9-other-queer-saints_n_1129804.html; Leslie Feinberg, *Transgender Warriors: Making History from Joan of Arc to Dennis Rodman* (Boston: Beacon Press, 1996).

43. Mark Twain, "Joan of Arc," Directory of Mark Twain maxims, quotations, and various opinions, accessed January 18, 2017, http://www.twainquotes.com/JoanofArc.html.

Bibliography

Adams, Jeremy duQ and Bonnie Wheeler. "Joan of Arc: History, Literature, and Film. Superhero, Crazy Trans-Kid, Saint, of Fraud?" English 3371, History 3357. Accessed January 18, 2017. http://www.smu.edu/~/media/Site/mayterm/2015Syllabus/D-1153_ENGL_3371-HIST_3357_AdamsWheelerSyll.ashx?la=en;

Armitage, Shelley. Review of *Visions of the Maid: Joan of Arc in American Film and Culture* by Robin Blaetz, *Journal of American History* 90, no. 2 (September 2003): 676-677. Accessed January 16, 2017. Academic Search Premier, EBSCOhost.

Barson, Michael. "Cecil B. DeMille, American Film Director." *Encyclopaedia Britannica*. September 4, 2013. Accessed January 18, 2017. https://www.britannica.com/biography/Cecil-B-DeMille.

Castleberry, Kristi J. "Joan of Arc's Brief Life and Long Afterlife," River Campus Libraries, University of Rochester, 2009. Accessed January 18, 2017. http://www.library.rochester.edu/robbins/joanexhibition.

Cherry, Kittredge. "Joan of Arc: Cross-dressing warrior-saint." *Jesus in Love* Blog. Accessed January 18, 2017. http://jesusinlove.blogspot.com/2013/05/joan-of-arc-cross-dressing-warrior-saint.html.

Crowther, Bosley. "Ingrid Bergman Plays Title Role in 'Joan of Arc' at Victoria." *The New York Times*. November 12, 1948. Accessed January 18, 2017. http://www.nytimes.com/movie/review?res=9403E2D6143DEE3ABC4A52DFB7678383659EDE.

De Pisan, Christine. Verse XXXVI, Ditié de Jeanne d'Arc. Ed. Angus J. Kennedy and Kenneth Varty, trans. L. Shopkow. Oxford: Society for the Study of Medieval Languages and Literature, 1977. Accessed January 18, 2017. http://www.indiana.edu/~dmdhist/joan.htm.

Ebert, Roger. "Review of The Passion of Joan of Arc by Theordor Dreyer." February 16, 1997. Accessed January 18, 2017. http://www.rogerebert.com/reviews/great-movie-the-passion-of-joan-of-arc-1928.

Feinberg, Leslie. *Transgender Warriors: Making History from Joan of Arc to Dennis Rodman*. Boston: Beacon Press, 1996.

Foxwell, Elizabeth. "Saint, Soldier, Spirit, Savior: The Images of Joan of Arc." *Minerva* XII, no. 3 (September 30, 1994): 36. Accessed January 16, 2017. https://search.proquest.com/docview/222786451?accountid=8289.

France, Anatole. "Chapter XIV, The Trial for Relapse—Second Sentence—Death of the Maid." *The Life of Joan of Arc.* Trans. Winifred Stephens. London: John Lane Company, 1908. Accessed January 17, 2017. http://www.gutenberg.org/files/19488/19488.txt.

Freeman, James A. "Joan of Arc: Soldier, Saint, Symbol—of What," *Journal of Popular Culture* 41, no. 4 (August 2008): 601-634. Accessed January 16, 2017. Academic Search Premier, EBSCOhost.

Gabel, Mathias and Carlyn Iuzzolino, trans., "Concluding Document: Sentence of Rehabilitation." *Saint Joan of Arc's Trial of Nullification*, 1903. Accessed January 17, 2017. http://www.stjoan-center.com/Trials/index.html#nullification.

_____. "Introductory Notes to the Nullification Trial." *Saint Joan of Arc's Trial of Nullification*, 1903. Accessed January 17, 2017. http://www.stjoan-center.com/Trials/index.html#nullification.

_____. "Second Process: The Relapse, Adjudication and Death Sentence," *Saint Joan of Arc's Trial of Condemnation,* 1903. Accessed January 17, 2017. http://www.stjoan-center.com/Trials/index.html#nullification.

Joan of Arc. *DC Memorialist.* Accessed January 18, 2017. http://dcmemorialist.com/joan-of-arc/.

Joan of Arch Robusto Connecticut. Thompson Cigar. Accessed January 18, 2017. https://www.thompsoncigar.com/product/JOAN-OF-ARCH-ROBUSTO-CONNECTICUT/94816.uts.

"Her Voices." *Portraits of a Saint.* Accessed January 18, 2017. http://saint-joan-of-arc.com/voices.htm.

Margolis, Nadia. "Joan of Arc from Medieval Europe to Modern America: A Visual History." Lecture at Farnsworth Art Museum, recorded April 14, 2016. Accessed January 18, 2017. https://vimeo.com/163032863.

Michelson, Noah. "Joan of Arc and 9 Other 'Queer' Saints." *The Huffington Post.* December 6, 2011.Accessed January 18, 2017. http://www.huffingtonpost.com/2011/12/05/joan-of-arc-and-9-other-queer-saints_n_1129804.html;

Pennington, Ken. "History 401: Joan of Arc." Accessed January 18, 2017. http://classes.maxwell.syr.edu/his401/index.htm

Shakespeare, William. *Henry VI*, Part 1, Act I, Scene V. Accessed January 18, 2017. http://shakespeare.mit.edu/1henryvi/full.html.

Shaw, George Bernard. *Saint Joan: A Chronicle Play in Six Scenes and An Epilogue*. 1924. Accessed January 18, 2017. http://gutenberg.net.au/ebooks02/0200811h.html.

Sollier, Joseph. "Felix-Antoine-Philibert Dupanloup." *The Catholic Encyclopaedia* Vol. 5. New York: Robert Appleton Company, 1909. Accessed January 18, 2017. http://www.newadvent.org/cathen/05202a.htm.

Taylor, Larissa Juliet. "Joan of Arc, The Church, and the Papacy, 1429-1920." *The Catholic Historical Review* 98, no. 2 (April 2012): 217-240. Accessed January 17, 2017. https://search-proquest-com.ezproxy1.apus.edu/docview/1013675739? accountid= 8289.

"The Beautification and Canonization of Saint Joan of Arc." Joan Directory. Accessed January 18, 2017. http://www.jehannedarc.org/canonization.html.

Thurston, Herbert. "St. Joan of Arc," *The Catholic Encyclopaedia*, Vol. 8. New York: Robert Appleton Company, 1910. Accessed January 17, 2017. http://www.newadvent.org/cathen/08409c.htm.

Twain, Mark. "Joan of Arc." Directory of Mark Twain maxims, quotations, and various opinions. Accessed January 18, 2017. http://www.twainquotes.com/JoanofArc.html.

Across the Etowah and into the Hell-Hole: Johnston's Lost Chance for Victory in the Atlanta Campaign

Greg A. Drummond

Despite being one of the more important campaigns of the American Civil War, the Atlanta Campaign has been somewhat underrepresented throughout the literature on the subject. While this oversight has been somewhat rectified in light of the sesquicentennial celebrations, most of these writings have focused on either the major battles that happened from late June 1864 through the fall of Atlanta or on the various commanders of the campaign. Nearly forgotten amongst all of this is the fighting that took place on the country crossroads and in the deep forests near Dallas, Georgia between 25 May and 4 June 1864. It was during this period of fighting that the Atlanta Campaign went from a series of quick flanking maneuvers to a constant daily grind of skirmishes and entrenchment, with little respite from weather-induced misery and the constant fear of death from an enemy one could not see. It was during this time that Confederate commander Joseph Johnston had the best chance to turn back the invasion of Georgia headed by Union general William T. Sherman. Johnston was able to effect a major change in the tempo and character of the campaign in the fighting around Dallas. However, his failure to contest Sherman's crossing of the Etowah River and his inability to stop the Union general from reconnecting with an unbroken Western & Atlantic Railroad ensured that the Confederates lost their best chance at stopping the invasion of Georgia.

The Armies Face Off

Going into the Atlanta Campaign, both commanders knew they faced a herculean task. Johnston's challenge when he took over the Army of Tennessee in December 1863 was to stop the much stronger Union forces from passing into Georgia and taking Atlanta, a city of just over 22,000. Atlanta, an important rail hub for the South and home to a number of mills and ammunition factories, was a vital strategic target.[1] However, following the disastrous battle at Missionary Ridge outside of Chattanooga, Tennessee the previous year, there was much work to do to ensure a strong fighting force for the Army of Tennessee. When Johnston took over, he inherited a severely demoralized and weakened force which he immediately set about drilling and preparing for the coming campaign, but with a strength of around 38,000 men, he realized he had to find more men before a campaign could be launched. By the end of April, he had collected a force of nearly 60,000 effective men and 154 cannon. General Leonidas Polk reinforced him with an additional 15,000 at Resaca.[2] While not a match in size for their foe, it was still a formidable force.

The Confederate Army of Tennessee, as it stood on the eve of the campaign, was a quite capable military force. It consisted of three corps of infantry, Lieutenant General William J. Hardee with four divisions, Lieutenant General John B. Hood with three divisions, Lieutenant General Leonidas Polk with two divisions, and a cavalry corps under Major General Joseph Wheeler with three divisions.[3] Johnston's constant drilling in the winter after taking command had a noticeable effect on Confederate morale, and the once demoralized forces were ready to fight once more.

Figure 1. General Joseph Johnston, C.S.A.
Photograph by Mathew Brady. National Archives.

Johnston knew, since he was facing a much larger force, that he would have to conserve his forces throughout the coming campaign. In order to combat the difference in manpower he had to adopt a Fabian-like strategy in which he would pull back behind strong entrenchments and try to entice Sherman to attack on his terms. When successful, it led to impressive Confederate victories.[4] Though Johnston was not averse to striking an isolated portion of the enemy lines, he preferred a defensive stance until Sherman could be defeated in battle and then chased back north. He refused the urging of Jefferson Davis and Braxton Bragg to strike into Tennessee before Sherman could advance, knowing he needed every man he could get for the coming campaign into Georgia.[5]

After President Abraham Lincoln called Ulysses S. Grant east from Chattanooga, Sherman was left in command of the western theater. Sherman had two roles to fill, first as commander of the Military Division of the Mississippi and

Figure 2. General William T. Sherman.
Photograph by Mathew Brady. National Archives

second as a field commander of three armies stationed at Chattanooga. Besides Sherman's previous command of the Army of the Tennessee, now commanded by Major General James McPherson and consisting of three corps, Sherman also had at his disposal the four corps of Major General George Thomas's Army of the Cumberland and the Army of the Ohio, which consisted of one corps under Major General John Schofield—all told around 100,000 men.[6] Sherman had a nearly two -to-one advantage in men and he planned to use that advantage to crush the enemy.

Sherman's campaign served two major purposes in the Union war effort. Not only was it meant to destroy the Army of Tennessee and end it as an effective fighting force, the offensive into the heart of Georgia was meant to take out as much of the South's ability to wage war as possible, weakening both Johnston's and Robert E. Lee's ability to continue fighting.[7] Sherman knew that attacking Johnston in his fortified positions was a futile effort, so from the beginning he followed a strategy of flanking the Confederate forces and forcing them to pull back or risk being cut off from their supply lines. Sherman had one major weakness, though. He was advancing into hostile territory with only a single supply line, the Western & Atlantic Railroad, of which he said after the war that the "Atlanta Campaign of 1864 would have been impossible without that road."[8] As future events would point out, Sherman needed the railroad. When he was not able to pull back quickly to it after attempting a flanking maneuver, things would become a near disaster.

To the Etowah

It is safe to say that up to the point where Sherman crossed the Etowah River, the Atlanta Campaign had gone completely in his favor. Beginning on 7 May 1864, the three Union armies under Sherman's command had forced Johnston out of several strongly entrenched positions with minimal casualties and at a frightening speed. Though Sherman's initial plan was to have the Army of the Tennessee march on Rome, Georgia while his other two armies held the Confederate forces at their heavily fortified positions outside the town of Dalton along Rocky Face Ridge, he instead sent this army through an undefended gap in the mountains of north Georgia, known as Snake Creek Gap. Had McPherson and his army gone through the gap to capture Resaca, Johnston would have been completely cut off from Atlanta. McPherson, however, felt he was in danger trying to go through the gap and stopped to fortify the entrance, alerting Johnston to his presence. This maneuver forced Johnston to pull back from Dalton during the night of 12 May to protect the Western & Atlantic Rail Road, which served as Johnston's lifeline just as much as it did Sherman's.[9] With this, Johnston began his backwards march through Georgia.

The town of Resaca was the next scene of conflict in the campaign. Johnston was able to once again create a strong fortified position here, especially with the arrival of Leonidas Polk's men. On 14 May, Sherman launched a strong attack at the Confederate center at Resaca, while sending Thomas Sweeney's division from the XVI Corps to the south to flank Johnston's army. The following

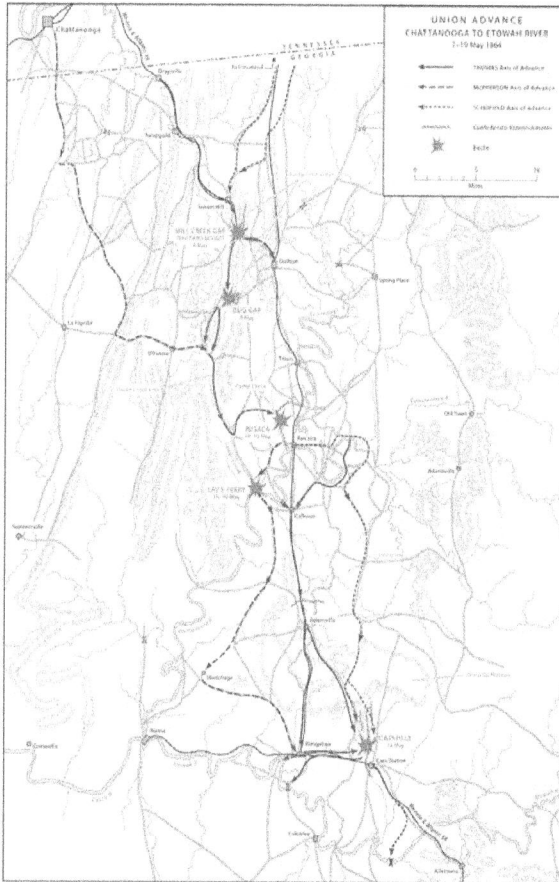

Figure 3. Union Advance from Chattanooga to the Etowah River. Map by J. Britt McCarley, United States Army Center of Military History

day, he sent Joseph Hooker's XX Corps to attack the Confederate right as Sweeney's men crossed the Oostanaula River at Lay's Ferry.[10] The fighting at Resaca was intense. Johnston's men were able to break up each attack, and even attempted to counterattack the Union left. According to historian Earl J. Hess, the fighting around Resaca turned into a "slugging match" between two entrenched armies. However, even with intense artillery fire throughout much of the battle, Sherman was able to slip men from a single division around the left flank of the Confederate forces. Once again, Johnston felt he had to withdraw from a strong position.[11] Without a decisive victory, Sherman had forced Johnston backwards.

Following Resaca, Johnston pulled back to the Cassville line. He sent Hood and Polk directly to Cassville and dispatched Hardee and Wheeler's cavalry to Cassville via Kingston, a move that forced Sherman to split his forces.[12] With Sherman's forces split, Johnston had a chance to strike out on the offensive himself. He planned for Hardee to quickly swing back to Cassville and with the Army of Tennessee reunited attack one part of the split Union army. Hood received faulty intelligence that foiled the plan, as it caused him to fall back at a critical moment.[13] Johnston's chance to attack had passed, and as the Federal army moved in he pulled back again, giving up even more territory.

Across the River

Johnston began to pull back again, leaving Cassville on the night of 19 May, and burning the railroad and road bridges as he left the area.[14] After crossing the river and leaving it undefended, Johnston made his way to a previously prepared position at Allatoona Pass, one of the strongest positions occupied by either side during the campaign. The state of Georgia created Allatoona Pass specifically for the Western & Atlantic Railroad, and Johnston felt that he had finally found a location that would force Sherman to attack him in a strong defensive position.[15] Johnston's plan, however, did not work out as he wanted, as Sherman did the unthinkable. Sherman had visited the area in 1844 and was familiar with its defensive capabilities.[16] If Sherman was able to get behind the Confederate army he could sever the Confederate supply line and take out Johnston's troops, but this would require leaving the protection of a long but stable supply line. The rewards were potentially great, but the risk was too. By leaving his supply line, Sherman ensured that he only had a limited amount of time and resources to achieve his goals before he was stuck without food for his army.

Sherman took several days to prepare for his movement to flank Allatoona Pass. He arrived at his headquarters in Kingston on 20 May and began to prepare for the upcoming movement. Over the next couple of days, Sherman ordered all sick and wounded men to the rear. He required that the troops gather twenty days' worth of supplies and that they forage for fresh meat and vegetables. However, he did not allow indiscriminate pillaging of the populace.[17] He then began deliberations on where his men would cross and how his supply line would remain properly defended from the constant threat of Confederate cavalry.

Sherman knew he needed to continue to protect his supply line, but he also realized he needed to find a replacement for the detachments of infantry necessary for this task. Leaving those already performing this task in place, he directed Brigadier General John E. Smith to move his division from Alabama toward Kingston, Georgia via Rome.[18] With his supply line protected from enemy cavalry, he then turned his attention to how he would get his large body of men across the Etowah River. Sherman, in the interest of ensuring that his armies kept out of each other's way on the march, had them stationed at three separate areas while preparing for the crossing. The Army of the Ohio, along with Stoneman's cavalry, was encamped at Cassville Depot, the Army of the Cumberland was near Cassville, and the Army of the Tennessee was stationed in Kingston. He stationed additional troops at Rome under Brigadier General Jefferson C. Davis.[19] Sherman commanded that all the armies prepare to move out on 23 May.

With this large number of men, Sherman had to devise a plan to cross the Etowah at a limited number of points against an unknown level of resistance from Johnston's forces. Sherman set the town of Dallas, Georgia as the next target for his forces. Dallas was a crossroads town approximately fourteen miles south of the Etowah and sixteen miles to the west of the important town of Marietta, Georgia, the next target of the Union advance.[20] In a great stroke of luck, Sherman's men were able to save two bridges across the river from destruction at the hands of the retreating Confederates, bridges that would prove to be instrumental in allowing Federal forces to cross. McPherson took his men across one of these, Wooley's Bridge, and proceeded on the longest march of Sherman's troops, moving southwest through Van Wert and then approaching Dallas from the west, bringing up Sherman's right. Thomas, minus Hooker's XX corps and occupying the center of Sherman's march, used Gillem's Bridge and a nearby ford to cross, moving south to Dallas through Euharlee and Stilesboro. On the left of Sherman's army was Schofield's Army of the Ohio and Stoneman's cavalry, with instructions to cross a pontoon bridge near one of the bridges destroyed by Johnston and protect the flank of the army closest to the Confederate positions at Allatoona, though Hooker's corps delayed their crossing. Hooker decided that Sherman must have wanted him to get across as fast as possible, so he took the pontoon bridge when it was empty. This left Schofield hours behind schedule.[21]

Most of these groups were across the river by the evening of 23 May and on their way toward Dallas. Sherman was confident of his success after finding the river crossing generally uncontested. On 23 May, he sent several pieces of correspondence in which he mentioned the expectations of a quick and successful movement. To Major General Francis P. Blair in Huntsville he stated that all of his forces were in motion toward Marietta, which he felt would force Johnston back to the Chattahoochee River just outside of Atlanta.[22] He would not reach Marietta until he forced Johnston from the slopes of Kennesaw Mountain in early July. In a ciphered message sent the same day, Sherman called the Etowah the "Rubicon of Georgia" and let it be known the Union forces would "swarm along the Chattahoochee in five days," a goal he would not reach for another six weeks.[23] Sherman felt that he had the advantage of Johnston, who had so far shown an ability to pull out of a compromised position and reinsert the Confederate forces between Atlanta and the invaders. Sherman could not have been more wrong.

Though the crossing had been mostly uncontested, Johnston had scouts stationed along the river reporting on Union movements. While he would later mention in his official report of the campaign that crossing the Etowah and letting the enemy cross unmolested was a major regret, it did allow him to move quickly to block Sherman's advance toward Dallas.[24] Johnston used his cavalry to keep watch, and by the time the first units began to move on 23 May, they had informed him of the movement. The Confederate commander was able to ascertain easily that the only place for Sherman to head was Dallas and he immediately began preparing troops to move out. By the evening of 23 May Johnston had sent out both Hardee and Polk's corps, leaving Hood to protect Allatoona in case Sherman had used some of his men to feint to the west while then moving for the strong position on the rail line.[25]

Johnston also decided to make aggressive use of his cavalry forces. He sent Wheeler's corps back across the river to harass the Federal rear at Cartersville, and used William Jackson's division to skirmish with the advancing Union troops. While Wheeler was unable to destroy enough rail to compromise Union supply lines, he was able to capture or destroy one hundred supply wagons and beat up the regiment guarding them. Jackson, on the other hand, retreated from a confrontation at Burnt Hickory with Union troops under Thomas, who was able to capture a letter from Johnston stating he was moving to block Sherman's advance.[26] Sherman disregarded the letter as a bluff, something he would later come to regret.

With Johnston pulling troops out of Allatoona Pass, Sherman had once again forced the southern army out of a strong position. However, as Johnston was

54

operating on interior lines, while Sherman swung out wide through the countryside, the Confederate commander was able to react quickly to the Union advance. Johnston benefitted from the terrain of the area as well. After leaving the mountains in the first days of the campaign, the two armies had moved into a region that had decent roads, and hilly, but generally navigable terrain. Once across the Etowah, this changed greatly. By 24 May, the Union forces had entered densely wooded terrain of which Sherman later recalled as "difficult" and barren of forage and useable roads.[27] This worked to the advantage of the Confederates, for the roads they were using were in much better shape.

On 24 May, Johnston realized the logical place for Sherman's forces to rendezvous was Dallas and made a catastrophic error. Instead of leaving at least a small garrison force at Allatoona, he ordered all of Hood's corps to the west behind the rest of the Confederate forces.[28] About this time, Sherman was working to reconnect all of his forces together to push eastward from the Dallas area toward Marietta and the Western & Atlantic. The pieces fell in place for a clash in the woods, one that those who fought through it remembered for its ferocity.

Fighting in the Hell Hole

Upon arriving in Dallas, Johnston began situating his forces to block Sherman's advance. Hood took up position on the Confederate left at New Hope Church, Polk took the center position, and Hardee held the right, just east of Dallas.[29] Once in place, the Confederates furiously began digging in for the attack they knew was on the way. Early that afternoon, just hours after Hood took up position, Hooker, as the lead element of the Army of the Cumberland, led his troops in fighting that was so severe that one Federal division commander later said his whole division went through their allotment of 60 rounds of ammunition during the fight.[30] Despite a strong showing by the Union forces, Hood's corps was able to repulse the enemy with heavy losses. Hooker's men had suffered 1,500 casualties to Hood's 500, with the Union forces falling back as a thunderstorm set in over the battlefield.[31] While both armies spent the following day building trenches, Sherman was on the verge of unleashing a full attack on Confederate positions.

Sherman was quite frustrated by this point. Not only had the Confederates blocked the way toward the Chattahoochee River and the city of Atlanta once again but Sherman had also left his supply line to move across country and was beginning to feel the pinch. On 27 May, Sherman decided he would make one last attempt to push around the right flank of the rebel army and that afternoon began the battle of Pickett's Mill. Sherman sent two divisions well to the right of what he thought was Johnston's forces and got a rude surprise in the form of Major General Patrick Cleburne's division.[32] Heavy fighting broke out in the midst of the Georgia wilderness, as well as another thunderstorm. As the initial attack broke down, reinforcements rushed in to help the faltering Union advance, but to no avail. The Confederates badly bloodied the Union forces, costing them around 1,600 men that day. The loss so upset Sherman that he never mentioned the battle in his official reports or in his memoirs after the war.[33] Sherman was ready to pull back to his supply lines, but before he could, one more action occurred. This time it was the Confederate's turn to blunder.

Johnston had finally stymied Sherman in the Georgian wilderness and felt the time was right to attempt an offensive maneuver of his own. Johnston had figured out that Sherman would be attempting to move back toward his supply lines and ordered Hardee to attack McPherson's Army of the Tennessee at the first sign of movement from the Federal troops. On the afternoon of 28 May, Hardee ordered three divisions to charge the Federal works in a disastrous attack that cost Johnston between 1,000 and 1,500 men for no real gain.[34] While this attack cost the rebels about as many men as the Federals had lost days before at New Hope Church, the effect was much greater on the smaller force. One brigade, known as the "Kentucky Orphan Brigade," lost so many men in this attack on McPherson that the unit disbanded following the campaign.[35]

This attack would have one slightly positive effect for the southern army though. It forced Sherman to hold his position for another couple of days due to the threat of further Confederate attack.[36] With his move away from the railroad to the west, Sherman had turned Johnston out of his strong position at Allatoona Pass. However, Johnston had managed to wreak a couple of severe defeats on Sherman. As the war entered the month of June, the armies would slow even more and the fighting would come to a crescendo.

Sherman Moves to Acworth

Johnston had succeeded in stopping Sherman's easy advance on either Marietta or the Chattahoochee and had inflicted a number of casualties on the Union forces. In the end, he had not forced a decisive battle that would turn back the invasion of Georgia. With the inability of the Union forces to find a way to flank either side of the Confederate lines Sherman began the painstaking task of working his way back to his supply line, and just in time. Though Sherman had brought enough supplies to last him for twenty days with allowances made for foraged material, the difficulty of travelling across the backcountry roads and lack

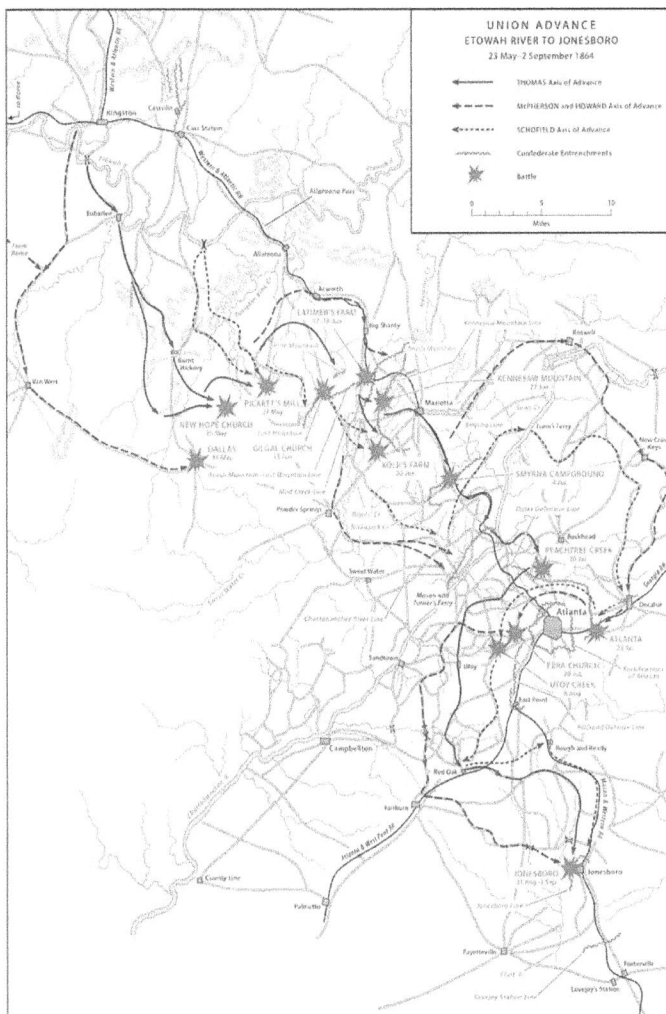

Figure 4. Union Advance Etowah River to Jonesboro. Map by
J. Britt McCarley, United States Center of Military History.

of inhabitants in the area meant that those supplies had begun to run out by the first
of June. As early as 27 May, just four days after crossing the Etowah, soldiers were
reduced to half rations and livestock, including horses, were dangerously low on
fodder.[37] It would still be eight days before Sherman's army would reconnect with
the rail line at Acworth.

The attack of 28 May compelled the Union forces to hold their lines in case an all-out Confederate assault came as they were pulling out for their move back toward the railroad. To accomplish this movement, Sherman began slowly moving his men to the northeast by extending entrenchments. The Confederates followed closely along and continued the constant skirmishing that had come to define this part of the campaign. Johnston noticed the beginning of this movement on the 27th, but it was not long before the manpower of the Union began to make itself felt. Unbeknownst to Johnston, Federal cavalry took Allatoona Pass unopposed on 31 May, opening Sherman's supply line, and the Union commander would make the former Confederate stronghold into a supply depot to help fuel his march on Atlanta.[38]

On 1 June, it became apparent that Union troops were beginning to outpace Confederate efforts. By 4 June Johnston had settled into his next defensive position on a line running from Lost Mountain on the left, across Pine Mountain, and ending on Brush Mountain to the right. Johnston once again pulled back from the enemy.[39] This ended the fighting during this portion of the campaign, allowing Sherman to consolidate control over an area south of the Etowah and set up his next movements toward Atlanta.

The fighting along the Dallas line was some of the fiercest seen by many of these soldiers. While there were some discernible battles, such as the actions at New Hope Church and Pickett's Mill, there was constant skirmishing up and down the line. Troops on both sides of the fighting found the action around Dallas to be taxing. One Union soldier described it as "probably the most wretched week" of the Atlanta Campaign.[40] With such terrible conditions, it is no wonder the soldiers, especially those of the Union forces, gave the area the nickname the "Hell Hole."

Several factors combined to create this horrendous atmosphere. The first was the challenging terrain. Nearly every account of this portion of the campaign mentioned how hard it was to travel through this area or even see the enemy. Reports from Oliver O. Howard after the action at Pickett's Mill described the terrain as "dense forests and thicket jungles, over country scarred by deep ravines," with visibility reduced to no more than a few yards on either side.[41] It is little wonder that in attempting to outflank the Confederate forces that day the Union troops instead ran into a bloodbath. Sherman also noted the difficulty of the terrain on more than one occasion. In his memoirs he said the area around Dallas was "very obscure" and "mostly in a state of nature" and noted that although he visited every sector of the Union line during this part of the campaign he rarely saw more than a handful of Confederate troops.[42] In addition to not being able to see the enemy, it was also quite easy to get lost. Artillerymen from one Union battery recall getting so mixed up on their march that they almost walked straight into Confederate lines with their guns and gear.[43]

In addition to challenging terrain, both armies had to contend with terrible weather. Beginning on 24 May it started raining nearly every day, with many days bringing the type of violent thunderstorms that frequently occur in the south during summer. One Union soldier described the storm following the battle at Pickett's Mill as "a furious storm, the rain came down in torrents, the lightning was blinding" and apparently the rainwater was collecting so fast that one man mentioned to his officer they could swim across the lines to fight the enemy.[44] With the addition of violent weather to the constant threat of bullets from a hidden enemy, it is not surprising that the name "Hell Hole" stuck. One Confederate surgeon mentioned in his diary that by 2 June, the fighting had continued for a week straight through rain and thunder, and the fighting was so terrible that he discovered one Union corpse with forty-seven balls lodged in his body.[45]

Johnston's Last Chance

Many historians who have studied this part of the Atlanta Campaign tend to write it off as something of an aside, perhaps because there was no decisive battle fought or clear winner. Prior to the crossing of the Etowah, the sides clashed at the Battle of Resaca and engaged in clear and decisive movements. After Sherman resumed his march south, the Union and Confederates met at the Battle of Kennesaw Mountain and in the contest for Atlanta.

A closer look, however, reveals much more. From the start of the campaign, Sherman's armies vastly outnumbered the Confederate forces. As the two armies approached Dallas though, the disparity in numbers became much tighter. Conditions forced Sherman to leave detachments along the Western & Atlantic Railroad, as well as to garrison captured cities, while Johnston gathered those he had sent to guard the other end of the same rail line. This meant that as the two armies met along the Dallas line Sherman had an effective strength of around ninety-two thousand men and Johnston had seventy thousand, a ratio of 1.3 to 1 in favor of the Union.[46] At no other point in the Campaign were the numbers to be so close. According to Sherman, on 5 June, the day after arriving at Acworth, he received a number of reinforcements which more than equaled the number of troops lost during the fighting in the Hell Hole.[47] If any time had been right for a major battle in the open field, this would have been it.

Besides not bringing the campaign to a decisive battle, Johnston made a number of mistakes that would prevent victory. One, as previously mentioned, was allowing Union troops to cross the Etowah River uncontested. While the high ground at Allatoona presented an excellent defensive position, Johnston should have realized from the tempo of the campaign up to that point that Sherman would be wary of attacking such a heavily fortified position. Had Johnston spread his army out and guarded the southern bank of the Etowah there is a good chance that the action would have stalled Sherman for weeks without being able to cross. The terrain to the Union's left was very mountainous and rough making a full-scale flanking maneuver of a river position nearly impossible, especially since the Allatoona Mountains overlooked the river. Had Sherman swung out around the Confederate left he would have had to go even further from his supply lines than he did going for Dallas.

Johnston made an even more egregious error by pulling all of Hood's corps out of Allatoona Pass and moving them to the Dallas line. Had he left even a single division at this location it would have presented a serious challenge to Sherman's cavalry forces. This in turn would have forced the Union commander to either mount a full-scale assault on the fortified position, with the added danger of the rest of Johnston's army to the rear, or else pull back above the Etowah to regain his supply lines. Johnston however performed in his usual manner and pulled back in the face of a challenge, deciding that protecting Marietta and the approaches to Atlanta was a safer decision than forcing his opponent back.

Despite this, Johnston's efforts along the Dallas line did produce some major results. He was able to inflict a number of casualties on the Union forces, a number just north of three thousand. While these numbers do not approach the level of casualties inflicted by Lee during the campaign in Virginia, such as the two-week period at Cold Harbor where the Union forces under Grant suffered the loss of about twelve thousand men, it reflects the much different nature of the fighting in Georgia.[48] Johnston was also able to slow Sherman to a crawl. Where before the crossing Sherman was covering miles a day, the Confederate actions around Dallas forced him to hold the same positions for nearly a week before he could even consider moving back toward his supply lines. This injected some much-needed morale into the Southern army. A Confederate surgeon notes that during this period the troops came to realize that Johnston's constant retreats had nothing to do with cowardice. When there was fighting the southern forces were dealing major blows, however, in their view, Sherman refused to fight.[49] Though the Confederate forces would have an impressive, though meaningless victory, at Kennesaw Mountain in late June, they lost their best chance of stopping Sherman when they allowed him to return to an unbroken rail line at Acworth. The rest of the campaign became a slow fade into defeat for the Army of Tennessee and the city of Atlanta.

Notes

1. Bruce Catton, *The American Heritage Picture History of the Civil War* (New York, NY: Bonanza Books, 1982), 481.

2. Earl J. Hess, *Kennesaw Mountain: Sherman, Johnston, and the Atlanta Campaign* (Chapel Hill, NC: University of North Carolina Press, 2013), 1.

3. David J. Eicher, *The Longest Night* (New York, NY: Simon and Schuster, 2001), 496.

4. U.S. War Department, *Official Record of the War of the Rebellion,* Series 1, vol. 38, part III, 619. (hereafter cited as *OR*).

5. Daniel J. Vermilya, *The Battle of Kennesaw Mountain* (Charleston, SC: The History Press, 2014), 30.

6. Eicher, *The Longest Night*, 696-697.

7. *OR,* Series I, vol. 38, part 1, 3.

8. "The Mountain Campaign in Georgia," *The Hocking Sentinel* (Logan, OH), February 25, 1886, accessed January 25, 2017, http://chroniclingamerica.loc.gov/lccn/sn85038119/1886-02-25/ed-1/seq-2/.

9. Vermilya, *The Battle,* 34.

10. Ibid, 38.

11. Hess, *Kennesaw Mountain*, 3.

12. Vermilya, *The Battle*, 39.

13. *OR*, Series I, vol. 38, part III, 616.

14. *OR*, Series I, vol. 38, part I, 65.

15. Vermilya, *The Battle of Kennesaw*, 41.

16. William T. Sherman, *The Memoirs of General W. T. Sherman* (New York, NY: Library of America, 1990), 511.

17. Albert Castel, *Decision in the West: The Atlanta Campaign of 1864* (Lawrence, KS: University Press of Kansas, 1992), 214-215.

18. Ibid., 214-215.

19. Sherman, *The Memoirs*, 511.

20. Castel, *Decision in the West*, 218.

21. Jeffrey S. Dean, *The Hell-hole in Georgia: Sherman vs. Johnston* (Westminster, MD: Heritage Books, 2006), 2-6 and Castel, *Decision in the West*, 217.

22. *OR*, Series I, vol. 38, part 4, 298.

23. Ibid., 299

24. *OR*, Series I, vol. 38, part 3, 616.

25. Dean, *The Hell-hole*, 8.

26. Ibid., 8.

27. *OR,* Series I, vol. 38, part 1, 60.

28. Dean, *The Hell-hole*, 8.

29. Castel, *Decision in the West*, 221.

30. Vermilya, *The Battle*, 42-43.

31. Ibid., 43.

32. Ibid., 46.

33. Ibid., 47.

34. Ibid., 48.

35. Philip L. Secrist, "Cobb County in the Atlanta Campaign," Civil War Trust, accessed January 25, 2017, http://www.civilwar.org/battlefields/kennesawmountain/kennesaw-mountain-history-articles/cobbcountysecrist.html.

36. Vermilya, The Battle of Kennesaw, 48.

37. Ibid., 47 and Chauncey H. Cooke, "Letters of a Badger Boy in Blue: The Atlanta Campaign," *The Wisconsin Magazine of History*, September 1, 1921, 21, accessed December 14, 2016, https://archive.org/details/jstor-4630341.

38. Castel, *Decision in the West*, 251.

39. Joseph E. Johnston, *Narrative of Military Operations: Directed, During the Late War Between the State* (New York, NY: D. Appleton and Co., 1874), 335, accessed December 12, 2016, https://archive.org/details/narrativeofmilit00john.

40. Richard M. McMurry, *The Road Past Kennesaw: The Atlanta Campaign of 1864* (Washington, DC: United States Department of the Interior, 1972), 21, accessed December 12, 2016, https://archive.org/stream/roadpastkennesaw00mcmu#page/n3/mode/2up.

41. Castel, *Decision in the West*, 230.

42. Sherman, *The Memoirs*, 512-514

43. Thaddeus C. Brown, Samuel J. Murphy, and William G. Putney, *Behind the Guns: The History of Battery I, 2nd Regiment, Illinois Light Artillery* (Carbondale, IL: Southern Illinois University Press, 2000), 94, accessed September 28, 2016, http://site.ebrary.com/lib/apus/detail.action?docID=10555641.

44. Dean, *The Hell-hole*, 28.

45. Enoch L. Mitchell, "Letters of a Confederate Surgeon in the Army of Tennessee to His Wife," *Tennessee Historical Quarterly* 5, no. 2 (June 1946): 169, accessed September 28, 2016, http://www.jstor.org/stable/42620894.

46. Dean, *The Hell-hole*, vi.

47. *OR,* Series I, vol. 38, part 1, 61.

48. National Park Service, "Cold Harbor," Richmond National Battlefield Park, accessed February 3, 2017, https://www.nps.gov/rich/learn/historyculture/cold-harbor.htm.

49. Mitchell, "Letters of a Confederate," 167.

Bibliography

Brown, Thaddeus C., Samuel J. Murphy, and William G. Putney. *Behind the Guns: The History of Battery I, 2nd Regiment, Illinois Light Artillery.* Carbondale, IL: Southern Illinois University Press, 2000. Accessed September 28, 2016. ProQuest Ebrary.

Castel, Albert. *Decision in the West: The Atlanta Campaign of 1864.* Lawrence, KS: University Press of Kansas, 1992.

Cooke, Chauncey H. "Letters of a Badger Boy in Blue: The Atlanta Campaign." *The Wisconsin Magazine of History,* September 1, 1921, 63-98. Accessed December 14, 2016. https://archive.org/details/jstor-4630341.

Dean, Jeffrey S. *The Hell-hole in Georgia: Sherman VS. Johnston.* Westminster, MD: Heritage Books, 2006.

Eicher, David J. *The Longest Night: A Military History of the Civil War.* New York, NY: Touchstone, 2001.

Hess, Earl J. *Kennesaw Mountain: Sherman, Johnston, and the Atlanta Campaign.* Chapel Hill, NC: University of North Carolina Press, 2013.

Johnston, Joseph E. *Narrative of Military Operations: Directed, During the Late War Between the States.* New York, NY: D. Appleton and Co., 1874. Accessed December 12, 2016. https://archive.org/details/narrativeofmilit00john.

McMurry, Richard M. *The Road Past Kennesaw: The Atlanta Campaign of 1864.* Washington, DC: United States Department of the Interior, 1972. Accessed December 12, 2016. https://archive.org/stream/roadpastkennesaw00mcmu#page/n3/mode/2up.

Mitchell, Enoch L. "Letters of a Confederate Surgeon in the Army of Tennessee to His Wife." *Tennessee Historical Quarterly* 5, no. 2 (June 1946): 142-81. Accessed September 28, 2016. http://www.jstor.org/stable/42620894.

National Park Service, "Cold Harbor." Richmond National Battlefield Park. Accessed February 4, 2017. https://www.nps.gov/rich/learn/historyculture/cold-harbor.htm.

Secrist, Philip L. "Cobb County in the Atlanta Campaign." Civil War Trust. Accessed January 25, 2017. http://www.civilwar.org/battlefields/kennesawmountain/kennesaw-mountain-history-articles/cobbcountysecrist.html.

Sherman, William T. *The Memoirs of General W. T. Sherman.* New York, NY: Library of America, 1990. *The Hocking Sentinel* (Logan, OH). "The Mountain Campaign in Georgia." February 25, 1886. Accessed January 25, 2017. http://chroniclingamerica.loc.gov/lccn/sn85038119/1886-02-25/ed-1/seq-2/.

U. S. War Department. *The Official Record of the War of the Rebellion: A Compilation of the Official Records of the Union and Confederate Armies.* 128 parts in 70 vols. and atlas. Washington: Government Printing Office, 1880-1901.

Vermilya, Daniel J. *The Battle of Kennesaw Mountain.* Charleston, SC: The History Press, 2014.

Cape Esperance: The Misunderstood Victory
of Admiral Norman Scott

Jeffrey A. Ballard

Sons of heroes, call forth the steel!

—Ossian

On the night of 8-9 August 1942, a combined Australian-American naval force, screening the amphibious landings in the Southern Solomon Islands, was completely surprised and thoroughly defeated by a numerically inferior Imperial Japanese naval force. The loss of Allied ships and sailors was unprecedented. The Battle of Savo Island was the worst defeat in United States Navy history and remains so today. During the 103-minute battle, 1,023 Americans and Australian sailors were killed and 709 wounded.[1] The next morning, one light and four heavy cruisers dotted the sea floor between Savo Island, Guadalcanal, and Florida Island. Thereafter, this body of water earned the nickname "Iron Bottom Sound" because compass needles quivered as ships passed over the accumulated mass of iron at the bottom.

One month later, Rear Admiral Norman Scott defeated a surprised Imperial Navy cruiser-destroyer force off Cape Esperance with the loss of only a single destroyer. There seemed no doubt that this reversal after the August defeat was an unqualified victory for the Navy, but this writer asserts it was not. South Pacific Commanders thought so, however, and dogmatically adopted Scott's tactics in order to snatch more quick victories on the contentious waters around Guadalcanal.

In the long run, however, the legacy of Scott's "victory" did more harm than good. The month after Cape Esperance, the fortunes of war reversed, and on 12-13 November, the Navy suffered intolerably once again. This night, four destroyers and a light cruiser joined the graveyard of ships below Savo Sound, and 739 lives, including two admirals, would be lost in pursuit of a second Cape Esperance.[2] Unquestioning repetition of Scott's tactics persisted throughout the Guadalcanal Campaign, into the New Georgia Campaign, and until the third quarter of 1943. As such, the misunderstood lessons of Cape Esperance were a contributing cause to the loss of more than a dozen ships and the deaths of many thousands of sailors, including Scott's own, in November 1942.[3]

Battle Narrative

The root cause of all the battles in the South Pacific during the fall and winter of 1942 was Japanese reaction to the American assault in the Southern Solomon Islands (7-8 August). Imperial General Headquarters was slow to react, believing the American landing was simply a raid on the unfinished airfield on Guadalcanal, and once destroyed, the Americans would withdraw. Imperial Navy estimates that less than two thousand US Marines had landed on the island supported this assumption, but the actual number was five and a half times that.[4]

In the first weeks of August, the Japanese took steps to retake the airfield and were bloodily repulsed. Repeatedly, Imperial Army commanders ordered poorly coordinated frontal assaults against the heavy weapons of the First Marine Division's perimeter. On the 21st they initiated a second effort to retake the airstrip, renamed Henderson Field by the Americans. Once again, without sufficient troops or coordination, their attempt to penetrate the Marine lines from across the Tenaru River failed.

In the final days of August, Imperial Naval Headquarters finally realized the danger posed by the Allied landings in the lower Solomons. Tokyo deferred the pending New Guinea offensive and redirected the 2nd (Sendai) Division to Guadalcanal. This strategic shift was significant because it elevated defense of the Solomon Islands above the capture of the Papuan Peninsula and further delayed a potential Japanese invasion of Australia.[5]

Unlike the Army, the Imperial Navy's reaction to the Allied landings in the Solomons was swift and decisive. The Combined Fleet, including three carriers and three battleships, sortied from Truk in the Caroline Islands, in an attempt to force the United States into a decisive battle that they hoped would drive the Americans to a negotiated peace. Imperial Navy preparations did not go unnoticed, however, and Australian Coastwatchers and Allied reconnaissance aircraft reported on its movements to Pacific Fleet headquarters in Hawaii. Commander-in-Chief Pacific Fleet (CINCPAC), Admiral Chester W. Nimitz, countered the advance with three carriers, resulting in the Battle of the Eastern Solomons, 24 August 1942. The Japanese lost light carrier *Ryujo* but inflicted heavy damage on the fleet carrier *Enterprise*.

On 11 October, at 1347, a B-17 from the 11th Bombardment Group (Heavy) observed a Japanese convoy tearing down the "Slot" less than one-hundred miles from Guadalcanal.[6] The USAAF aircrew erroneously reported the "Tokyo Express" as being composed of two cruisers and six destroyers.[7] In fact, the Army pilots had spotted Rear Admiral Takaji Joshima's "Reinforcement Group," which consisted of two seaplane tenders, not cruisers, and six destroyers that transported advance elements of the 2nd Division and much of its heavy equipment.

Several hours behind Joshima, but part of a separate operation, was Cruiser Division 6; heavy cruisers *Aoba*, *Kinugasa*, and *Furutaka*. On 9 October, the Eighth Fleet headquarters at Rabaul dispatched the veterans of Savo Island to bombard Henderson Field two nights later. With the airfield out of commission, Joshima could make good his escape on the 12th. Commanded by Rear Admiral Aritomo Goto since the Battle of the Eastern Solomons, the cruisers, screened by two destroyers, remained undetected by Allied reconnaissance aircraft or Coastwatchers at dusk.

With three new American task forces in the area, Commander South Pacific Fleet (COMSOPAC), Vice Admiral Robert L. Ghormley, felt sufficiently equipped to challenge any Japanese reinforcement of Guadalcanal. COMSOPAC, gifted by the arrival of the Army's American Division, ordered the 164th Infantry Regiment to reinforce the beleaguered First Division Marines on the island.

The nearest of Ghormley's units was Task Force 64.2, commanded by Rear Admiral Norman Scott, who flew his flag in the heavy cruiser *San Francisco*. COMTF64.2 had been present at Savo Island but was unengaged as commander of the Southern Force in light cruiser *San Juan*. Determined not to be surprised, as the Allies had been in August, Scott patrolled just north of the Rennell Islands, beyond the range of the big Japanese Kawanishi flying boats at Rabaul. He would, however, be ideally situated to intercept any Japanese advances.

After two days of uneventful cruising, TF 64.2 began its approach to Savo Island at 1600 on the 10th. Scott held COMSOPAC orders to "search for and destroy enemy ships and landing craft."[8] An hour later, Scott announced to Task Force Sugar his intention to engage the enemy just before midnight and repeated the enemy's strength as reported to him via short-range Talk Between Ships (TBS) radio.[9] At sunset (1815), Scott set Condition Readiness ONE and all hands went to General Quarters.[10] After rounding the northwest coast of Guadalcanal, TF 64.2 began to patrol north-northeast from a point north of Cape Esperance to Savo Island an hour before midnight (2300).[11]

Scott's ships assumed "formation DOG," the line-of-battle reminiscent of the Age of Sail. His cruiser division included the heavy cruisers *San Francisco* and *Salt Lake City* and the light cruisers *Boise* and *Helena* bracketed fore and aft by two divisions of destroyers. Captain Robert G. Tobin, Commander Destroyer Squadron 12 (COMDESRON12), led the column in flagship *Farenholt*, followed immediately by *Laffey* and *Duncan*. Destroyers *Buchanan* and *McCalla*, newcomers to the task force, followed *Helena*, the last cruiser in column.

Despite his awareness of Joshima's position, Scott miscalculated the enemy's arrival time. Consequently, he missed an opportunity to strike the Reinforcement Group, which was already unloading at various points along Guadalcanal's northern shore. He was, however, in a perfect position to strike Goto's unsuspecting "Bombardment Group."

At about 2200, Scott, expecting contact with the enemy within the hour, ordered his floatplanes aloft to spot for his cruisers.[12] The admiral, who knew the damage burning planes had caused at Savo Island, had already ordered his Curtiss SOC "Seagull" scout planes, except one per cruiser, to be flown-off to Tulagi. Additionally, Scott ordered all non-essential flammables be stowed or jettisoned. Ominously, *Salt Lake City's* plane crashed on takeoff when "a flare in the cockpit inexplicably ignited."[13] The flaming wreck threatened to give away the position of Task Force Sugar. Fortunately for the Americans, Joshima could not see the conflagration because of an intervening land mass and radioed Goto that the Sound was clear of Allied shipping. Joshima also failed to mention the presence of enemy scout planes that might have warned Goto of the American presence.

After sunset, all radar sets in the American formation were energized and active, sweeping their assigned sectors. At 2225, *Helena's* sensitive millimeter-wave (SG) radar registered Goto's formation bearing 315°T, distance 27,000 yards (15.33 miles) but failed to report the contact for 17 minutes.[14] The tactical situation was the reverse of that two months earlier at Savo, with the Americans aware of the approaching enemy and at battle stations, while the Japanese approached Guadalcanal unaware of the American presence and unprepared.

Getting uncomfortably close to the west coast of Savo Island, Scott countermarched to the southeast. At 2332 Scott ordered a column (follow-the-leader) turn of 180 degrees to port via TBS: "This is CTF. Execute to follow: left to course 230°" and thirty seconds later, "CTF. Execute."[15] Inexplicably the column split in two with *Farenholt* leading *Laffey* and *Duncan* in a wider arch. *San Francisco* and the remaining ships turned more tightly placing Tobin's destroyers between Scott and the approaching enemy. Tobin, realizing his predicament, ordered the former lead destroyers to increase speed, advance along the cruiser's starboard flank, and regain their position ahead of San Francisco.

Helena finally reported the contact to COMTF64.2, and *Salt Lake City* and *Boise* immediately concurred.[16] *Boise's* radio operator, however, reported the unidentified contact as five "bogies," and referenced a relative and not a true (magnetic) bearing.[17] *Boise's* use of the code word for an airborne contact and the illogical compass heading confused Scott.[18] With *San Francisco's* meter-wave (SC) radar turned off, the admiral was unable to verify that the contacts on *Boise's* screen were not Tobin's destroyers. He knew only that the destroyers were somewhere off his starboard side.

Unknown to both Scott and Tobin, *Duncan* had left the formation and was singlehandedly executing a torpedo attack on an enemy cruiser. *Helena*, *Boise*, and *Salt Lake City*, whose radar images were becoming clearer by the moment, did not believe that their contacts were American. At least one United States ship fired on *Duncan*, because she received multiple hits on her unengaged (opposite) side, meaning that the rounds were American and not Japanese.[19]

The countermarch had caused Scott to inadvertently cross Goto's "T," at the range of only 4,600 yards (2.61 miles).[20] COMTF64.2 could not have asked for a better firing solution, but blind to the fully developed radar plot, issued no orders. At 2345, *Helena's* skipper requested permission to commence firing and Scott responded "Roger" but the admiral had only meant to acknowledge *Helena's* last transmission.[21] *Helena's* first salvo committed the American fleet and within a minute, all of Task Force Sugar's guns were ablaze. While the cruiser's secondary batteries illuminated the Japanese with star shells, the American 6 and 8-inch main batteries poured fire into the unsuspecting Bombardment Group.

Moments before the Americans commenced hostilities, the ships in Goto's formation were preparing to begin the midwatch with Savo Island broad off their port bow.[22] CRUDIV6 (*Aoba*, *Kinugasa*, and *Furutaka*), less heavy cruiser *Kako*, which had been sunk by the American submarine S-44 on 10 August, departed Shortland Island at the southernmost point of Bougainville on 9 October.[23] To ensure the "Cactus Air Force" could not interfere with Joshima's escape, Goto intended to bomb Henderson field and ground her planes.[24] Goto had made this round trip once before, bombarding Lunga Point on Guadalcanal on 25 August. This action deprived the Marines of much needed sleep but he arrived too late to support the Imperial Army crossing the Tenaru.[25] Nevertheless, for his current mission, the destroyers *Fubuki* and *Hatsuyuke* screened Goto's heavy cruisers. Covering the 349 miles in two days, Goto would enter Savo Sound about midnight on 11 October, bombard the Marine position, and make good his escape before dawn.

As American salvos began to strike his force, Admiral Goto refused to believe battle was at hand. Like the Allied commanders at the Battle of Savo Island, the Japanese were completely unprepared and for six or seven crucial minutes, did not react.[26] Goto believed Joshima's destroyers were firing on him and signaled with his blinkers "I am *Aoba*" repeatedly making the flagship's bridge an instant target for American gunners.[27]

Aboard the San Francisco, *Helena's* unexpected commencement of hostilities caused the admiral genuine alarm. Scott nearly threw away the advantage of surprise when he ordered a ceasefire to check on the status of his destroyers. "How are you?" queried the admiral via TBS. Tobin replied he was fine but did not know who the cruisers were shooting at.[28] Scott ordered a resumption of fire at 2351, but only after *Farenholt* flashed recognition lights—green over green over white, in vertical line.[29]

The Office of Naval Intelligence's report described the situation after 2351 as being "so intense and the firing by all the ships so rapid and simultaneous that it is impossible to relate the events in any great detail or with a clear chronology."[30]

Unable to stop what he believed was friendly fire, Goto ordered a 180-degree column turn (instead of a simultaneous turn) to starboard to escape.[31] Such a turn caused each ship in the Japanese formation to pivot and reverse course in the same spot as the preceding. This made the Japanese easy targets and the Americans sank the *Fubuki* before it finished its turn. The blinking signal lights on the *Aoba* directed American gunfire that wrecked the bridge and mortally wounded admiral Goto. Rapid fire from the light cruiser's 6-inch guns and the rhythmic salvoes of the heavy cruiser's 8-inch main batteries sank the *Furutuka*. In the confusion, *Kinugasa* and *Hatsuyuki* inadvertently turned to port rather than starboard, and

Figure 1. The Japanese Heavy Cruiser, *Aoba,* photographed soon after completion, c. 1927-1929. Naval History and Heritage Command collection.

because the Americans concentrated on the closer ships, they escaped.

At precisely midnight, and with the Japanese in full retreat, Scott ordered a ceasefire and the flashing of recognition lights. *Boise* foolishly turned on its searchlights and received ten or eleven hits from the retreating Japanese, causing immense damage. The deluge caused one of *Boise's* magazines to explode, disabling all three forward turrets and the ship fell out of column to the port.[32] Quick action by *Salt Lake City* saved *Boise*, as it interposed itself between the stricken *Boise* and the retreating enemy. As a result, the heavy cruiser *Kinugasa* hit *Salt Lake City* with two 8-inch shells.[33] By twenty minutes after midnight, all radar screens were clear, and Scott called off the chase.

Analysis

The Battle of Cape Esperance was the second of five surface engagements between ships of the United States and the Imperial Japanese navies near the South Pacific island of Guadalcanal, Solomon Islands. The Japanese called the clash the Sea Battle of Savo Island, referencing the first surface action two months earlier.

Although COMTF64.2 prevented Goto from accomplishing his mission, the conduct of the battle was far from flawless. The botched countermarch highlighted Rear Admiral Richmond K. Turner's observation that "scratch teams performed poorly in stressful situations."[34] It was becoming apparent that ships in the combat zone had too little time for training, and the exercises Scott conducted while loitering near Rennell Island could not make up for years of neglect. The Americans overcame small errors such as the misuse of the term "bogie" and the usage of relative, rather than true (magnetic) readings but the battle showed the significance of these small errors. Captain Tobin, in his after-action report suggested that the code word "skunk" be used to describe an identified surface contact, and Nimitz ordered the change immediately.[35]

Norman Scott, a bona fide member of the Navy's "Gun Club," employed naval rifles to the exclusion of torpedoes in achieving his mission. Scott's battle plan specified that the cruisers were to employ "continuous fire against small ships at short range, rather than full gun salvos with long intervals."[36] Admiral William "Bull" Halsey, who succeeded Ghormley as COMSOPAC six days after the battle, was extremely impressed with *Helena* and *Boise's* machinegun-like fire of their 6-inch main batteries. The hyper-aggressive Halsey ordered "continuous fire," as opposed to measured "salvo fire," to become the fleet's standard operating procedure.[37] Halsey's judgement, which equated volume of fire with accuracy, was well intentioned but flawed. Navy gunnery studies, conducted after the New

Georgia Campaign, showed that of 4,591 6-inch shells fired, only one-quarter of one-percent (12) scored a hit.[38]

The battle drew attention to fire distribution as an emerging issue with radar-controlled gunfire. Although Scott's battle plan called for a normal distribution of fire (each ship fires on the vessel opposite it) all of Task Force Sugar's radar-directed gunners tended to fire on the ship with the most prominent radar signature.[39] Consequently, the two nearest ships with the most prominent signatures, *Fubuki* and *Furutaka*, received excessive fire. Both ships received devastating damage while the remaining enemy ships, except *Aoba*, escaped relatively unhurt. In all fairness to American gunners, the perpendicular orientation of the formations complicated target selection. Better fire discipline was required, to which CINCPAC subscribed "training, TRAINING and MORE T-R-A-I-N-I-N-G."[40]

Both Nimitz and his boss, Admiral Ernest J. King, Commander-in-Chief US Fleet (COMINCH), questioned Scott's choice of *San Francisco* as his flagship. On 9 August, Scott had selected the light cruiser *San Juan*, which was equipped with SG radar, so the admiral knew the millimeter-wave radar's surface search capabilities. At Cape Esperance, *San Francisco* used only its short-range Fire Control (FC) radar, which was not designed for surface search. For security reasons, *San Francisco* turned off its own SC set.[41] Thus, Scott relied on his seeing-eye-dogs *Helena* and *Boise*. Flying his flag on any of the three other cruisers, all equipped with SG radar, would have given the admiral immediate access to the complete radar picture and thus facilitated prompt decision-making.

The action also illustrated that the US Navy lacked sufficient surface warfare doctrine for light forces at night. To his credit, Scott made it up as he went along and his force generally

Figure 2. Rear Admiral Norman Scott. U.S. Navy photograph, now in the collections of the National Archives.

performed very well. In his endorsement of the COMTF64.2 after-action report,

Nimitz's greatest criticism, which would be largely unaddressed for another ten months, was the underutilization of Tobin's destroyers. CINCPAC cogently noted that "Of the 25 torpedoes carried by Tobin's destroyers that night, only seven had been fired (two from the *Duncan* and five from the Buchanan), none of which struck a target."[42] Scott's battle plan instructed only that the destroyers should "illuminate targets as soon as possible and to . . . fire torpedoes at large ships [from their position in the column]."[43] The admiral had no intention, and gave no order to Tobin to initiate a torpedo attack but instead, chose to use the DESRON12 ships defensively. Japanese and friendly fire alike pummeled *Duncan*, the only American destroyer to initiate an independent torpedo attack. It seems that within sixty days, South Pacific commanders had already forgotten that the Japanese Type 93 "Long Lance" torpedoes heavily damaged three of the four American heavy cruisers sunk at Savo Island, which was proving to be the killing weapon of surface warfare.

The Battle of Cape Esperance did demonstrate that the Navy was rectifying the errors of the August debacle. Scott, forewarned by effective aerial reconnaissance from Espiritu Santo-based Flying Fortresses, took measures that

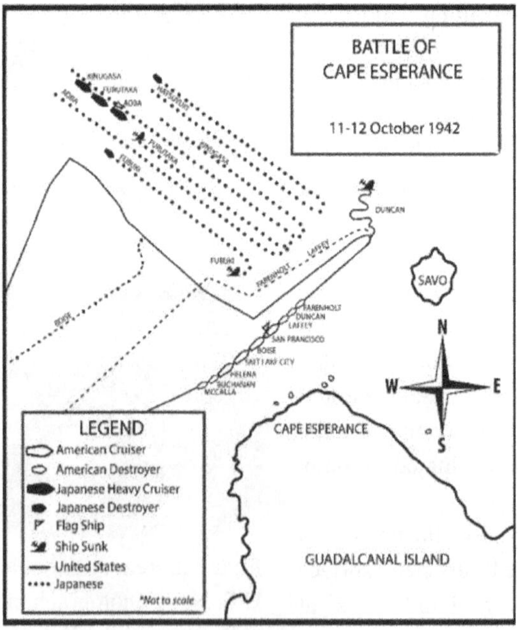

Figure 3. Battle of Cape Esperance. Map created by author.

Figure 4. *USS Duncan* (DD-485) underway in the south Pacific on 7 October 1942, five days before she was sunk in the Battle of Cape Esperance. Photographed from *USS Copahee* (ACV-12). U.S. Navy Photograph, from the collections of the Naval History and Heritage Command.

Savo Island commanders had not. The admiral drafted a cohesive battle plan and communicated it to TF 64.2 skippers two full days before the battle.[44] Aware that crew fatigue had been a major factor in the defeat two months earlier, Scott made sure his crews had ample time to take meals and ready their battle stations before calling them to General Quarters.

Scott strictly adhered to CINCPAC's new policies addressing the cause of the many fires triggered by Japanese shells and torpedoes in August. Nimitz concluded that the all-consuming fires aboard the Northern Group of heavy cruisers, (*Quincy*, *Vincennes*, and *Astoria*) were "due, in part, to the large amount of flammable materials on board, a consequence of the many years of peacetime cruising."[45] He then issued a fleet wide directive ordering the removal of unnecessary topside combustibles and unneeded observation aircraft from ships before going into combat.[46]

Finally, an important characteristic of Scott's success was that TG 64.2

met the enemy outside of Savo Sound, so its movements were not restricted by the surrounding islands. On the open waters, Scott maximized the effectiveness of his radar and prevented the Imperial Navy, which was proving to be an adept night fighting force, from hiding their silhouettes against Guadalcanal's high mountain range or the high volcanic cone of Savo Island.

Certainly, Cape Esperance was a shot in the arm for American morale, which had been in freefall since August. It is worth questioning whether Scott's tactics were worthy of the unquestioning duplication they received by South Pacific commanders, and if Cape Esperance was a lasting victory.

Like most every surface action in the Southern Solomon Islands, Cape Esperance was strategically inconclusive, because it did not award local naval superiority to either combatant. By dusk the following night, the Americans had virtually surrendered Iron Bottom Sound to the Imperial Navy. Scott did succeed in preventing the bombardment of Henderson Field that night, but four nights later the Marines would endure a hellish assault. During "The Bombardment," battleships *Kongo* and *Haruna* lobbed over nine hundred, 14-inch, high-explosive shells on Marine positions and the airfield. The cannonade destroyed forty-eight planes, killed forty-one men, and put gapping craters in the airfield that grounded the Cactus Air Force for more than a month.[47] The Imperial Navy took full advantage of the grounding and reinforced Guadalcanal with infantry, artillery, and heavy equipment, including tanks, in broad daylight. The sight of Japanese transports disgorging troops on the beach caused one exasperated Marine Colonel from First Division Headquarters to report "We don't know whether we'll be able to hold the field or not."[48]

Based on the after-action reports submitted by Scott's captains, Nimitz calculated that TG 64.2 had sunk three cruisers and five destroyers. In the CINCPAC's endorsement to King, Nimitz determined, "we administered as severe a defeat to them as they did to us in the earlier battle."[49] He concluded that with the advantage of surprise, like that enjoyed by the Japanese on the night of 8-9 August, "our light forces are equal or superior."[50] In reality, the damage inflicted by Scott was not comparable at all. In the summation, the American margin of victory was but one Japanese cruiser, making Cape Esperance a marginal victory for the USN. Damage to the surviving ships was about equal. *Boise* was forced to return to the United States for repairs on her three forward turrets and likewise *Aoba*, with her number 2 and 3 turrets disabled and her bridge wrecked, returned to Kure. Neither would return to action until spring 1943.

The October battle occurred far too soon after the Savo Island defeat to make any definitive judgements about Scott's tactics. Significant staff work was

Figure 5. *USS Boise* (CL-47) arrives at the Philadelphia Navy Yard, Pennsylvania, for battle damage repairs, November 1942. The damage she sustained resulted in a large fire that burned out her three forward 6/47 gun turrets and their ammunition spaces. U.S. Navy Photograph, National Archive.

required to analyze lessons learned from past operations, formulate recommendations, and make doctrinal changes. This lag meant that months passed between evaluation and implementation, causing recommendations to arrive too late to affect the outcome of subsequent battles. For example, the Navy did not release its official report on the Battle of Savo Island until May 1943, nine months after the action and four months after Guadalcanal was secure.[51]

Four major surface battles took place on or near Iron Bottom Sound during the period between Savo Island and the release of the "Hepburn Report." In almost every case, commanders emulated some or all of Scott's tactics. Though the actions foiled Japanese plans to either reinforce the Imperial Army or bombard Henderson Field, the cost in ships and lives was staggering. For example, by the time the Americans secured Guadalcanal in February 1943, the Japanese had sunk or severely damaged twelve of the fourteen heavy cruisers committed to the

Southern Solomons. *Salt Lake City* was the exception, and received only moderate damage during the 11 October battle.[52] In terms of lost ships and men, the final reckoning of the Guadalcanal Campaign was that the combatants losses were approximately equal, reinforcing the marginal nature of the tactical effort.[53]

In the final analysis, the Japanese defeat at Cape Esperance had more to do with their failures than with American successes. Goto had been surprised because, up to this point, the Navy had completely deserted the Sound at night. Japanese certainty that the Sound was free of Allied shipping was due to lack of vigilance and Joshima's failure to grasp the significance of cruiser floatplanes and report their presence to Goto. The Japanese would not likely make these mistakes again.

Scott's Legacy

As noted above, South Pacific commanders sought to repeat Scott's success for the remainder of the Guadalcanal Campaign and the first half of the New Georgia Campaign—often with calamitous results. One month after Cape Esperance, Rear Admiral Daniel J. Callaghan lead a cruiser-destroyer force in the Night Cruiser Action of 12-13 November. Within the confines of Savo Sound, the American column smashed headlong into the Japanese formation of two battleships, one heavy cruiser, and eleven destroyers. The engagement quickly degenerated into a "barroom brawl with the lights out"[54] as American and Japanese ships mixed like fish in a barrel. Point-blank gunfire on the flagship's bridge killed Callaghan and most of his staff.

Nimitz judged the action was a tactical victory, because like Cape Esperance, Callaghan prevented the bombardment of Henderson Field. The overoptimistic Naval Intelligence Branch estimated that Callaghan had sunk three cruisers, five destroyers, and that no enemy ship escaped damage.[55] In reality, Callaghan had damaged the two battleships, three destroyers, and had sunk two destroyers. The Americans lost the light anti-aircraft cruiser *Atlanta* and four destroyers. Due to heavy damage, both heavy cruisers *San Francisco* and *Portland* left the theater for repair. The only ship to escape unscathed was the destroyer *Fletcher*.

While it can be debated whether the results were worth the cost, there is little dispute that Callaghan fought this battle poorly. Although Scott, the victor of Cape Esperance, was present in his flagship *Atlanta*, he was junior to Callaghan, the Officer in Tactical Command (OTC). Callaghan, who had been Ghormley's chief of staff, was put to sea by Halsey's promotion to COMSOPAC and had little tactical command experience. Consequently, he imitated Scott's October tactics and in doing so, he repeated the errors of Cape Esperance and even magnified some.

Callaghan was roundly criticized for not issuing a battle plan, as Scott had done, and for not selecting a ship equipped with SG radar as his flagship. This night, however, the ships tracking the Japanese approach reported the contact immediately, but because he lacked the complete tactical picture, Callaghan squandered his radar advantage and failed to issue timely and succinct orders.[56]

Like Scott at Cape Esperance, Callaghan also failed to employ his destroyers effectively. Nimitz and King both censured Callaghan for repeating Scott's mistake of tying his destroyers to the cruiser line. King lamented deploying destroyers in this manner "unnecessarily exposed the destroyers to gunfire and prevented them from making a coordinated torpedo attack,"[57] adding "Destroyers are essentially an offensive weapon, particularly at night with their torpedoes."[58]

Collectively, the scratch team of seven destroyers from two different squadrons launched forty-nine torpedoes, but post-war records indicate they did not strike any Japanese ships.[59] Nonetheless, excessive American optimism claimed twenty-four torpedo hits. The Japanese, on the other hand, scored six hits on five ships, which contributed to the sinking of *Laffey*, *Cushing*, *Barton*, and *Monssen* and damaging the stern of *Portland*.[60]

Unlike his favorable assessment of the October battle, Nimitz criticized Callaghan for selecting the column formation and distributing destroyer divisions fore and aft of the cruisers. In this case, a thirteen-ship column proved unwieldy and difficult to maneuver. CINCPAC also wondered why the ships with SG radar were placed eighth and last in the column and not first and fifth.[61] Closing his report, Nimitz reiterated that the single biggest problem confronting the Navy in the Solomons was that his commanders continued to focus on naval gunfire, generally ignoring the offensive potential of their destroyers while simultaneously dismissing the effectiveness of the enemy's torpedoes.[62]

Vice Admiral William S. Pye, the President of the Naval War College, went so far as to say if Callaghan had survived, a court-martial was in order. Instead, both Callaghan and Scott received the Congressional Medal of Honor (posthumously).[63]

If Norman Scott was the disciple of Alfred Thayer Mahan's "Big Gun Navy" then Rear Admiral Willis A. Lee was his prophet. Not unexpectedly then, the Naval Battle of Guadalcanal was fought exclusively by the radar-controlled gunnery of his battleships *Washington* and *South Dakota*. The action was the Navy's first battleship versus battleship combat since Admiral Sampson fought the Spanish at Santiago, 3 July 1898. On the night of 14-15 November, Lee sank the battleship *Kirishima*, which brought with it the distinction of being the only battleship sunk by another battleship in the South Pacific theater.[64] Destroyer torpedoes holed battleships *Yamashiro* and *Fuso*, sunk at the Battle of Suriago Strait on 24-25 October 1944, before Admiral Oldendorf's battleships finished them off.

Based on available information, Naval Intelligence believed that Lee had defeated a superior force, sinking one battleship, three to five cruisers, and a dozen destroyers.[65] The truth was far less impressive. Actual Japanese losses were one World War I-era battleship and a destroyer. But once again, American claims of victory were substantiated because Henderson Field aircraft were flying again the next day. Lee was fortunate that his destroyers—and later *South Dakota*—drew the attention of the Japanese torpedoes, sparing the flagship any serious damage.

A gushing Halsey wrote that Lee's plan was "audaciously planned and executed."[66] Uncharacteristically, both Nimitz and King restrained their criticism. However, Nimitz did observe that if Lee's column had engaged the Japanese outside of the Sound, as Scott had done at Cape Esperance, the enemy would not have been able to approach from the radar shadow caused by Savo Island.[67]

Contrary to using his destroyers offensively, Lee used them as bait for Japanese torpedoes and only one of the four survived. Admiral Pye criticized Lee for this mistreatment, but the undisputed chairman of the Gun Club was not bothered by the censure. In Nimitz's report to King, he expressed, for the first time, his concerns about the American Mk.15 torpedo. He found the *Gwin's* inability to dispatch foundering *Benham* embarrassing.[68]

Except for Savo Island, the Battle of Tassafaronga was the Navy's worst surface defeat of the Pacific War. After a bright moon period, which suspended all but the most critical nocturnal visits to Guadalcanal, the Tokyo Express returned to the Sound with the waning moon. In the early hours of 1 December, eight Imperial Navy destroyers sailed deep inside the Sound and dealt a devastating blow to Rear Admiral Carlton Wright's numerically superior Task Force 67.

The Japanese skirted Tassafaronga Point to hide their silhouette in against Guadalcanal's 6,000 foot mountain range, but Wright's flagship *Minneapolis*, equipped with SG radar, detected the Japanese at a distance of 23,000 yards. The American battle line of four heavy cruisers and a light cruiser tracked the enemy as the two forces closed on reciprocal and nearly parallel courses. With a combined speed of thirty-two knots, the formations closed rapidly, and the range quickly fell below 10,000 yards (5.6 miles).[69]

For this mission, Halsey had assigned Wright the four destroyers of Destroyer Division 9 (Commander William M. Cole). Cole arranged his ships in a column 4,000 yards off *Minneapolis's* port bow in an attempt to address the underutilization of Seventh Fleet destroyers. Per Wright's battle plan, Cole was to deliver a torpedo attack and clear the gunnery range, thereby avoiding *Duncan's* fate. For their part, the cruisers were to withhold fire until the first American torpedo detonated.

A detached destroyer column dedicated to offensive action demonstrated progress but Cole was not free to initiate the attack and required an order from Wright to do so. For eight minutes, Wright hesitated, and Cole watched his ideal firing solution disappear before requesting permission to launch. Wright delayed again, wasting another six minutes before giving the order. The twenty-four torpedoes fired by DESDIV9 sped into an impossible tail chase because the Japanese were abaft the beam of the destroyers.

In the meantime, the cruiser's range to target fell well below the minimum range specified in Wright's battle plan and the admiral ordered his 6 and 8-inch guns to fire before all Cole's torpedoes had left their tubes. Now with ample warning, the Japanese immediately executed a counter-march and escaped, but not before firing twenty fast-running torpedoes of their own.[70] Wright would have done well to order a similar 180° turn because his cruisers sailed directly into the deadly spread of Japanese Long Lance torpedoes. All four TF 67 heavy cruisers were struck by at least one torpedo knocking off the bows of *Minneapolis* and *New Orleans* forward of Turret No. 2, holing *Pensacola* and sinking *Northampton*. Herculean effort by fleet tugs saved *New Orleans* and the flagship, but both returned to the United States for lengthy repairs. Only *Honolulu* and Cole's destroyers escaped undamaged. Destroyers *Lardner* and *Lampson*, attached to the force at the eleventh hour, fired a few ineffectual salvos, but kept their distance for most of the action lest they suffer the same fate as *Duncan*.

Nimitz believed Wright exaggerated when stating he had sunk two light cruisers and seven destroyers. Nevertheless, both Nimitz and King restrained their criticism. With some help from Naval Intelligence, CINCPAC revised the totals downward to four destroyers sunk and two others damaged, but even this was an exaggeration. TF 67 sank only a single destroyer and failed to damage any of the other seven ships present. This fact can be attributed to poor fire distribution, which had remained an issue since Cape Esperance, with all of Wright's cruisers firing on the hapless *Takanami*, the largest and brightest blip on their radar screen.

Wright received little criticism for his conduct of the battle even though his losses were disproportionate to the damage inflicted. Halsey was most displeased with Captain Cole for not launching his torpedoes at the optimal angle and range, but it was Wright and not Cole who caused the delay. Nimitz judged that, "the conduct of the battle was generally correct."[71] CINCPAC concluded his report, of what would be the final battle of the Southern Solomon Islands Campaign, by saying that the Japanese were more skilled in the use of guns and torpedoes. This conclusion was an oversimplification that gave little consideration to issues of leadership, doctrine, and the developing awareness of problems with the Mk.15 torpedo.

By 9 February 1943, the Japanese quietly completed their evacuation of Guadalcanal, and Halsey looked forward to resuming King's plan to neutralize the Japanese citadel at Rabaul. Lacking the amphibious resources to assault the Central Solomons for the time being, Halsey assembled an impressive array of naval power with which to "keep pushing the Japs around."[72]

Lee's *Washington*, three recently commissioned fast battleships, and two older battleships joined carriers *Enterprise* and *Saratoga* in the South Pacific. This gave Halsey mobility and striking power, but the confined waters of the New Georgia Sound would prove just as dangerous to the Navy's heavies as Iron Bottom Sound. The tip of Halsey's spear, therefore, would be Rear Admiral Waldon "Pug" Ainsworth's cruiser-destroyer Task Force 38.

When the American invasion of New Georgia finally came, on the last day of June 1943, the Japanese were unprepared. The Imperial Navy responded with the limited forces at their disposal resulting in two actions named the Battles of the Kula Gulf (5-6 July) and Kolombangara (12-13 July). Although considered minor naval actions compared to the colossal battles on Iron Bottom Sound, both are worthy of discussion because they demonstrate how the legacy of Cape Esperance persisted through the Guadalcanal Campaign and into the next.

Ainsworth's conduct of both battles resembled that of Scott's at Cape Esperance in most every way. Prior to each battle the admiral conducted a brief conference and presented the same battle plan with an A and B option. Neither option utilized the offensive capabilities of the destroyers assigned to his command. He did allow them to fire at targets of opportunity but only after gunfire, in full radar control mode, commenced. Before both battles, Ainsworth arrayed his force in column with destroyers fore and aft of the cruiser line. In both cases, he maneuvered to cap the enemy's T. Like Wright, Ainsworth failed to make significant course changes, after initial contact, and sailed into torpedo water.

Fortunately for the Americans, Japanese torpedo gunnery was uncharacteristically poor and only sank light cruiser *Helena* (Kula Gulf) and damaged *Honolulu*, *St. Louis*, and *Leander*, sinking destroyer *Gwin* at Kolombangara. Similar to Wright's assessment of his battle, Ainsworth was convinced he had won two major victories. In actuality, he had sunk only destroyer *Niizuki* (Kula Gulf) and the old light cruiser *Jintsu* (Kolombangara).

It appears that Ainsworth did not read any of the action reports of the battles on Savo Sound. Consequently, the admiral deviated little from Scott's conduct nine months earlier and duplicated many of the errors made previously. Despite being Commander of Destroyers in the Pacific for the first half of 1942, Ainsworth used his destroyers defensively like Scott at Cape Esperance. Ainsworth, like Scott and Lee, was a devotee of the naval rifle, and relied entirely on the high rate of fire and superior fire control of light cruisers *Honolulu*, *Helena*, and *St. Louis*, which overwhelmed the enemy's lead ships, demonstrating poor gunfire distribution.

Halsey was generally pleased with Ainsworth's performance and praised his battle-plan, although he had duplicated Scott's tactics, which were under heavy scrutiny in mid-1943. COMSOPAC criticized Ainsworth for "missing the 'golden opportunity'" to deliver an early torpedo attack.[73] He also repeated the mantra that destroyer commanders need freedom and lamented the missed offensive opportunities.[74] The torpedoing of all four of his cruisers was evidence that existing doctrine needed revision. Nimitz was less pleased with Ainsworth than Halsey. CINCPAC's main concern was the damage to the cruisers, as *Honolulu* and *St. Louis* lost their bows to torpedoes. They survived, but were out of the war for an extended period. Capping the T, while ideal for naval gunfire, provided a poor torpedo solution. Poor fire distribution under radar-controlled gunfire continued to be a problem.

Conclusion

While Admiral Scott's success at Cape Esperance was a much-needed boost to American morale, his victory had sinister consequences on the conduct of future operations. South Pacific Commanders strove to replicate his achievement by mirroring Scott's tactics, but Scott's feat was due to exigent circumstances, and this flawed their logic. The Americans caught Goto off guard because since the August battle they virtually abandoned control of Savo Sound to the Japanese every night. Consequently, the Navy's sudden reappearance completely surprised the Japanese. TF 64.2 also benefited from the fact that Joshima's exact position was unknown to Goto, causing him to withhold fire for six to seven crucial minutes, while he challenged the Americans with his desperate "I am *Aoba*" message. Neither circumstance would likely occur again.

The Navy's belief that Cape Esperance was a smashing success (rather than a marginal victory) reinforced the pre-war notion that gunfire alone would be the final arbiter in naval combat. Furthermore, it seemed to vindicate the Mahanian cult of the Big Gun as Scott "demonstrated his allegiance to this school of thought."[75] Consequently, the Americans continued to "concentrate on tactics designed to maximize the effectiveness of gunfire"[76] to the exclusion of a balanced surface warfare doctrine. The superiority of the "hammer and anvil" of gunnery and torpedo would be demonstrated at Vella Gulf (6-7 October 1943), improved at Cape St. George (24-25 November 1943) and perfected at Surigao Straight (25 October 1944).

It would be a year before anyone recognized the flaws in Admiral Norman Scott's victory, and because of this, the Navy lost indispensable ships and many hundreds of sailors. Had Scott survived the South Pacific Campaign there is every reason to believe that he would have been an agent of change, but the fact is he did not live to celebrate Thanksgiving 1942. As mentioned previously, friendly fire from the *San Francisco* killed Scott on 13 November and he posthumously received the Congressional Medal of Honor. Incidentally, in 1942, 13 November was a Friday.

Notes

1. Samuel Eliot Morison, *The Struggle for Guadalcanal: August 1942- February 1943*, vol. V of *History of the United States Naval Operations in World War II* (Boston: Little, Brown and Company, 1949), 63.

2. Richard B. Frank, *Guadalcanal: The Definitive Account of the Landmark Battle* (New York: Random House, 1990), 459–460.

3. James D. Hornfischer, *Neptune's Inferno* (New York: Bantam Books, 2012), 437.

4. Hornfischer, 44.

5. Adrian Stewart, *Guadalcanal: World War II's Fiercest Naval Campaign* (London: William Kimber, 1985), 75.

6. Chester W. Nimitz, CINCPAC Report, December 26, 1942, 2, Record Group 38, Box 19, National Archives II, College Park, MD.; The "Slot" was the nickname given the New Georgia Sound which was bordered by the two parallel island chains that made up the Solomon Islands.

7. Recognizing the danger posed by Allied airpower in the daylight, the Japanese transported troops to Guadalcanal in regular nightly destroyer runs, the frequency of which prompted American sailors and airmen to refer to these operations as the "Tokyo Express."

8. U.S. Navy. Combat Narratives: Solomon Island Campaign, Office of Naval Intelligence. IV *Battle of Cape Esperance*, 11 October 1942, 3, Washington DC: Office of Naval Intelligence, Publications Branch, 1 October 1943. No. 485.

9. Ibid., 6.

10. Ibid., 5.

11. Ibid.

12. Ibid., 7.

13. Ernest G. Small, *USS Salt Lake City* Action Report, October 19, 1942, 4, Record Group 38, Box 1390, National Archives II, College Park, MD.

14. Combat Narratives, 7.

15. Ibid., 7.

16. Ibid., 11.

17. Edward J. Moran, *USS Boise* Action Report, October 30, 1942, 4, Record Group 38, Box 1025, National Archives II, College Park, MD.

18. Norman Scott, Task Group 64.2 Action Report, October 22, 1942, 3, Record Group 38, Box 17, National Archives II, College Park, MD.

19. Morison, 161.

20. Crossing or capping the "T" was a tactic used in naval warfare where one line of ships passes in front of another at a right angle. This maneuver allows the crossing line to bring all their guns to bear while their enemy may only rely on their forward guns.

21. Scott, 4.

22. The watch was from midnight to 4 AM (0000-0400).

23. Raizo Tanaka, "Japan's Losing Struggle For Guadalcanal," United States Naval Institute Proceedings, 82 (July 1956): 699.

24. The Allied code word Cactus referred to Guadalcanal, so the mixed bag of Navy, Marine and USAAF aircraft which operated from Henderson Field were called the Cactus Air Force.

25. Morison, 73.

26. Matome Ugaki, *Fading Victory: The Diary of Admiral Matome Ugaki, 1941-1945* (Pittsburgh, PA: University of Pittsburgh Press, 1991), 237.

27. Ibid.

28. Charles H. McMorris, *USS San Francisco* Action Report, October 31, 1942, TBS Transmissions, unpaged, Record Group 38, Box 1396, National Archives II, College Park, MD.

29. Morison, 160.

30. Combat Narratives, 12.

31. A simultaneous turn is the opposite of the column turn (follow the leader) as all ships in the column initiate the turn immediately from their present position.

32. Moran, 11.

33. Small, 16.

34. Morison, 271.

35. Robert G. Tobin, COMDESRON12, Action Report, October 23, 1942, 60, Command File, World War II, Box 341, Naval Historical Center, Washington, DC Navy Yard.

36. Combat Narratives, 3.

37. William F. Halsey, Commander South Pacific, Second Endorsement of USS McCalla Action Report, January 8, 1943, 1, Record Group 38, Box 22, National Archives II, College Park, MD.

38. Vincent P. O'Hara, *The U.S. Navy Against the Axis: Surface Combat, 1941-1945* (Annapolis: Naval Institute Press, 2007), 318.

39. Combat Narratives, 3.

40. Chester W. Nimitz, CINCPAC Report, December 15, 1942, 16. Record Group 38, Box 19, National Archives II, College Park, MD.

41. McMorris, 11.

42. Frank, 297, 304.

43. Combat Narratives, 3.

44. Ibid.

45. Chester W. Nimitz, Pacific Fleet Confidential Letter 29CL-42, July 28, 1942, 1. Command File, World War II, Box 233, Naval Historical Center, Washington, DC Navy Yard.

46. Ibid.

47. Morison, 172-174.

48. Ibid., 175.

49. Chester W. Nimitz, CINCPAC Report, December 26, 1942, 6.

50. Ibid.

51. Arthur J. Hepburn, Report of the informal inquiry into the circumstances attending the loss of the *U.S.S. Vincennes, U.S.S. Quincy, U.S.S. Astoria*, and *H.M.A.S. Canberra*, on August 9, 1942, in the vicinity of Savo Island (Solomon Islands). May 13, 1943, 52. Record Group 38, Box 1727. National Archives II, College Park, MD.

52. Jeffrey A. Ballard, "Firing Point: The Evolution of U.S. Navy Destroyer Torpedo Attack Doctrine During Operation Watchtower, 1942-1943" (master's thesis, American Military University, 2015), 56.

53. Hornfischer, xix.

54. Hornfischer, 292.

55. Chester W. Nimitz, CINCPAC Report, December 28, 1942, 1, Record Group 38, Box 19, National Archives II, College Park, MD.

56. Ernest J. King, Battle Experience, March 15, 1943, Chapter 20, 10, Record Group 334, National Archives II, College Park, MD.

57. Ernest J. King, Battle Experience, March 25, 1943, Chapter 28, 11, 18 & 37, Record Group 334, National Archives II, College Park, MD.

58. Ibid.

59. Ballard, 43.

60. Ibid.

61. Ibid., 44.

62. Chester W. Nimitz, CINCPAC Report, February 18, 1943, 20, Record Group 38, Box 19, National Archives II, College Park, MD.

63. William S. Pye, Comments on the Battle of Guadalcanal, June 5, 1943, 3, Record Group 38, National Archives II, College Park, MD.

64. Hornfischer, 366.

65. Ballard, 48.

66. William F. Halsey, Report of Night Action, Task Force 64, March 2, 1943, 1, Record Group 38, Box 25, National Archives II, College Park, MD.

67. Jeff T. Reardon, "The Evolution of the U.S. Navy into an Effective Night-Fighting Force During the Solomon Islands Campaign, 1942-1943" (PhD. diss, the College of Arts and Sciences of Ohio University, Athens, OH, 2008), 7-49.

68. Chester W. Nimitz, CINCPAC Report, March 18, 1943, 2, Record Group 38, Box 20, National Archives II, College Park, MD.

69. Morison, 297-298.

70. Ibid., 302.

71. Chester W. Nimitz, CINCPAC Action Report, February 15, 1943, 15, Record Group 38, Box 19, National Archives II, College Park, MD.

72. Theodore Roscoe, *United States Destroyer Operations in World War II* (Annapolis: Naval Institute Press, 1953), 216.

73. William F. Halsey, First Endorsement on CTG 36.1 Action Report of August 3, 1943, September 10, 1943, 3, Record Group 38, Box 140, National Archives II, College Park, MD.

74. Ibid.

75. Reardon, 67.

76. Nimitz, CINCPAC Report, December 28, 1942, 8.

Bibliography

Ballard, Jeffrey A. "Firing Point: The Evolution of U.S. Navy Destroyer Torpedo Attack Doctrine During Operation Watchtower, 1942-1943." Master's thesis, American Military University, 2015.

Frank, Richard B. *Guadalcanal: The Definitive Account of the Landmark Battle.* New York: Random House, 1990.

Halsey, William F. Commander South Pacific, Second Endorsement of USS McCalla Action Report, January 8, 1943. Record Group 38, Box 22, National Archives II, College Park, MD.

_____. First Endorsement of CTG 36.1 Action Report of August 3, 1943, September 10, 1943. Record Group 38, Box 140, National Archives II, College Park, MD.

_____. Report of Night Action, Task Force 64, March 2, 1943. Record Group 38, Box 25, National Archives II, College Park, MD.

Hepburn, Arthur J. Report of the informal inquiry into the circumstances attending the loss of the *U.S.S. Vincennes, U.S.S. Quincy, U.S.S. Astoria*, and *H.M.A.S. Canberra*, on August 9, 1942, in the vicinity of Savo Island (Solomon Islands), May 13, 1943, Record Group 38, Box 1727, National Archives II, College Park, MD.

Hornfischer, James D. *Neptune's Inferno: The U.S. Navy at Guadalcanal.* New York: Bantam Books, 2012.

King, Ernest J. Battle Experience, March 15, 1943. Record Group 334, National Archives II, College Park, MD.

King, Ernest J. Battle Experience, March 25, 1943. Record Group 334, National Archives II, College Park, MD.

McMorris, Charles H. USS San Francisco Action Report, October 31, 1942, TBS Transmissions, unpaged. Record Group 38, Box 1396, National Archives II, College Park, MD.

Moran, Edward J. *USS Boise* Action Report, October 30, 1942. Record Group 38, Box 1025, National Archives II, College Park, MD.

Morison, Samuel Eliot. *History of United States Naval Operations in World War II.* Volume V: *The Struggle for Guadalcanal, August1942-February 1943.* Boston: Little, Brown and Company, Inc., 1949.

Nimitz, Chester W. Pacific Fleet Confidential Letter 29CL-42, July 28, 1942. Command File, World War II, Box 233, Naval Historical Center, Washington, DC Navy Yard.

_____. CINCPAC Report, December 15, 1942. Record Group 38, Box 19, National Archives II, College Park, MD.

_____. CINCPAC Report, December 26, 1942. Record Group 38, Box 19, National Archives II, College Park, MD.

_____. CINCPAC Report, December 28, 1942. Record Group 38, Box 19, National Archives II, College Park, MD.

_____. CINCPAC Report, February 15, 1943. Record Group 38, Box 19, National Archives II, College Park, MD.

_____. CINCPAC Report, February 18, 1943. Record Group 38, Box 19, National Archives II, College Park, MD.

_____. CINCPAC Report, March 18, 1943. Record Group 38, Box 20, National Archives II, College Park, MD.

O'Hara, Vincent P. *The U.S. Navy Against the Axis: Surface Combat, 1941-1945.* Annapolis: Naval Institute Press, 2007.

Pye, William S. Comments on the Battle of Guadalcanal, June 5, 1943. Record Group 38, National Archives II, College Park, MD.

Reardon, Jeff T. "The Evolution of the U.S. Navy into an Effective Night-Fighting Force During the Solomon Islands Campaign, 1942-1943" PhD. diss, The College of Arts and Sciences of Ohio University, Athens, OH, 2008.

Scott, Norman. Task Group 64.2 Action Report, October 22, 1942. Record Group 38, Box 17, National Archives II, College Park, MD.

Small, Ernest G. *USS Salt Lake City* Action Report, October 19, 1942. Record Group 38, Box 1390, National Archives II, College Park, MD.

Stewart, Adrian. *Guadalcanal: World War II's Fiercest Naval Campaign.* London: William Kimber, 1985.

Tanaka, Raizo. "Japan's Losing Struggle For Guadalcanal," Part I, *United States Naval Institute Proceedings,* 82 (July 1956): 687-699.

Tobin, Robert G. COMDESRON12, Action Report, October 23, 1942. Command File, World War II, Box 341, Naval Historical Center, Washington, DC Navy Yard.

Roscoe, Theodore. *United States Destroyer Operations in World War II.*
    Annapolis: United States Naval Institute, 1953.

Ugaki, Matome. *Fading Victory: The Diary of Admiral Matome Ugaki, 1941-1945.*
    Pittsburgh, PA: University of Pittsburgh Press, 1991.

U.S. Navy. Combat Narratives: Solomon Island Campaign, Office of Naval
    Intelligence. IV *Battle of Cape Esperance, 11 October 1942.* Washington
    DC: Office of Naval Intelligence, Publications Branch, 1 October 1943.
    No. 485.

"Died on the Field of Honor, Sir." Virginia Military Institute in the American Civil War and the Cadets Who Died at the Battle of New Market: May 15, 1864

Lew Taylor

The Shenandoah Valley of Virginia, known as the "Breadbasket of the Confederacy," is home to the Virginia Military Institute. Located in Lexington, Virginia, VMI played a significant role in the American Civil War—from the execution of John Brown in 1859 to the disbanding of the Corps of Cadets during the fall of Richmond in 1865. The Corps, consisting of young men between the ages of fifteen and twenty-five, served on active duty with the Confederate Army several times during their years at VMI but no one could have predicted the events of May 11-15, 1864, when the Corps marched from their campus in Lexington into history at the Battle of New Market. During this battle, ten cadets paid the ultimate price. Today, over one hundred fifty years later, new cadets report to New Market to learn about the sacrifices made in 1864, and walk where the cadets of 1864 fought and died. Roll call taken on the anniversary of the Battle of New Market includes the names of those who died. A cadet, designated as their representative, responds to the names of the fallen with, "Died on the Field of Honor, Sir."

In 1818, the Commonwealth of Virginia established an arsenal in the town of Lexington and stationed militia guards there to guard the arsenal and its contents. The people of Lexington, a sleepy little valley town, and home to Washington College, had no problem with the arsenal itself. However, the off-duty behavior of the militia concerned them. "The discipline was strict, but could not prevent [the soldiers] from making use of their leisure in ways that made them a very undesirable element in the population of a small town."[1]

It was not long after the establishment of the arsenal that talk began about "converting the installation into an educational institution, with the students as its caretakers."[2] In the 1830s, a Lexington merchant by the name of Hugh Barclay visited the United States Military Academy at West Point. Impressed by the curriculum, the level of discipline and the morals of the students enrolled there, he returned to Lexington and began talking up the old idea of turning the arsenal into an educational facility. At a meeting of the Franklin Society—a local literary and debating society—Barclay asked, "Would it be politic for the State to establish a military school, at the Arsenal . . . in connection with Washington College, on the plan of the West Point Academy?"[3] The members of the society voted unanimously to support the establishment of such a school. It was not long after this that John Thomas Lewis Preston—a Lexington attorney who was present at the meeting—began writing a series of articles for the Lexington Gazette to raise more support for the idea.

After extensive lobbying by Preston and other supporters of the school, the Virginia legislature passed legislation. This reorganized the arsenal as a "military school of Washington College" with "academic and military systems based on the École Academy [in France] and West Point."[4] In April of 1836, eighteen years after the establishment of the arsenal, the Virginia Military Institute became a reality. École and West Point served as a model for the school, per the legislation, but it was not going to be an exact copy. From the beginning, VMI looked at the military aspect of the school as "only a means to an end: their goal was not the production of career military officers, but rather the molding of young personalities."[5] Military training, while an integral part of the cadets' experience, would not interfere with the student's academic studies. The objective of the school "was not to fit its graduates for a single profession . . . but to prepare young men for the varied work of civil life. . . . The military feature, though essential to its discipline, is not primary in its scheme of education."[6] While the legislation establishing VMI claimed it would be a part of Washington College, the school's trustees said that the state legislature did not have the authority to link the two schools. As a result, VMI never became a part of Washington College.

The faculty and administration of VMI, like those of the other military schools of the South, were reasonably sure that secession was coming, and began to prepare for it. Even though the education at VMI was not supposed to be a military education, Major Raleigh E. Colston feared the cadets would be unready when inevitably called into service. Colston, a professor of Military Strategy, said, "While the cadets knew all there was to know about drilling squads, companies, or battalions, they did not know much about caring for men on the march or in camp."[7] While some dismissed Major Colston's concerns, they turned out to be valid as the cadets were called into military service.

The first military service performed by the cadets of VMI took place in 1859 at the execution of John Brown in Charles Town, Virginia. The governor of Virginia, John Letcher, concerned that supporters of Brown might attempt to free him or in some other way disrupt the execution, called on VMI to provide additional military presence in Charles Town. The superintendent of VMI, Francis Henney Smith, was directly in charge of the execution itself, and ordered eighty-five cadets, along with two artillery pieces under the joint command of Majors

William Gilham and Thomas J. Jackson, to proceed to Charles Town. Jackson, in a letter to his wife, described the positioning of the cadet contingent: "My command was still in front of the cadets, all facing south. One howitzer I assigned to Mr. Trueheart on the left of the cadets, and with the other I remained on the right. Other troops occupied different positions around the scaffold, and altogether it was an imposing, but very solemn, scene."[8]

When Virginia finally passed an ordinance of secession, thousands of men flooded into Richmond to volunteer for military service. The task of turning these poorly armed, untrained men into a legitimate army fell to the cadets of VMI. While this was not their preferred assignment, the cadets believed that they were capable of accomplishing it. In April of 1861, 185 cadets were busy at Camp Lee, Virginia—a camp of instruction set up at the state fairgrounds in Richmond—training the new recruits.

Superintendent Smith offered to form the cadets into a battalion for active service with the Confederate Army. However, the government rejected the offer, as they believed the cadets would be far more valuable as officers. Many of the cadets resigned from the Institute and enlisted in various units throughout the Confederate Army, dropping the enrollment to less than thirty students. At this point (July 1861), the remainder of "the cadets were dismissed with directions to report when further orders were issued."[9] Following the Battle of First Manassas, Robert E. Lee said, "We never wanted the advantages of military instruction more than now and the Virginia Military Institute is the best and purest fountain from which we can be supplied."[10] The Virginia Military Institute now carried the responsibility of training officers in the Confederate Army. In January of 1862, the Virginia Military Institute reopened.

It was not long before the Confederacy once again called the cadets into active service. Under the command of Colonel Scott Shipp, the Commandant of Cadets, they supported the forces of General Thomas J. Jackson, their former artillery instructor, during the McDowell Campaign in May of 1862. The cadets pursued Federal troops through the mountains of western Virginia but were not engaged in any battles of the campaign. At one point, Jackson called the cadets to the front to be part of the burial detail. "He wanted to dispel any notions of battlefield glory the young soldiers may have brought with them from the Institute."[11]

In the fall and early winter of 1863, the Corps took the field again. This time it was to defend against the raids of General William Averell around Roanoke and Salem, Virginia, just south of the Institute. Again, while pursuing the Federals, the cadets did not engage in any battles. However, this was soon to change. The next time they took the field, it would not be to train or to pursue the enemy, but to engage them on the field of battle.

In the spring of 1864, the Shenandoah Valley once again became the scene of active military actions. On May 9, Union Major General Franz Sigel began his march southward from Winchester, Virginia on the way to Staunton where he planned to destroy the railroads leading into the valley. The Confederacy did not have a significant force stationed in the valley at that time, so a makeshift force of about five thousand men under the command of Major General John C. Breckenridge countered Sigel. The force consisted of Breckenridge's two brigades of about 2500 men, a small cavalry force under the command of Brigadier John D. Imboden, and the combined reserve and home guard detachments from Augusta, Rockingham, and Rockbridge counties. "Desperate to put troops in the field, the Confederates even prevailed upon the 247-man corps of cadets from the Virginia Military Institute."[12]

Late in the evening of May 10, 1864, the cadets received their orders to march the following morning. It was just before daybreak on the morning of May 11, 1864, when the drums began to beat the long roll on the parade grounds at VMI. All but the forty-seven youngest cadets, who remained in Lexington to guard the school, began to emerge from their barracks to assemble into their companies. The gray uniforms of these cadets, all between the ages of fifteen and twenty-four, were spotless. The brass buttons shone brightly in the light of the lanterns surrounding the parade ground. After officers inspected each cadet to see that he had the proper equipment, the column moved out in perfect order through the town of Lexington and onto the Valley Turnpike for the march north.

The "seed corn of the Confederacy," as they were called by Jefferson Davis, formed into four companies and marched eighty miles north along the Valley Pike to New Market, and onto the front lines, becoming part of a charge through a muddy field, into the fire of both artillery and infantry and onto the pages of history. General John C. Breckinridge knew that his forces were outnumbered, and he "neither desired nor planned to put the cadets into the battle."[13] It was soon obvious that he had no choice. The Union army was pushing the Confederate center and Breckinridge issued a command that stated, "Put the boys in, and God forgive me for the order."[14]

As Colonel Keith Gibson wrote in his article "Virginia Military Institute at War," "Fate, more than planning, brought the young soldiers to the Confederate line at a critical moment on the New Market battlefield. After heavy Union artillery fire punched a hole in the center of the Confederate line, the Cadet Corps moved from its reserve position into the breach then spearheaded the Confederate infantry assault across a rain-soaked wheat field."[15] That field is now known as the "field of lost shoes" due to the number of shoes pulled off by the deep mud.

When the smoke cleared, this relatively insignificant battle began to grow in importance. Not only had the Confederates, with their hastily assembled army, captured a large number of prisoners, as well as six pieces of artillery, they had sent Sigel and his forces retreating down the Valley. The cadets were excited about the outcome. Derided by veterans a day earlier because of their young age, clean uniforms, and shiny buttons, these young men had now shown their fighting prowess. At the height of the battle, they breached the Union line,[16] charged a Union position, and captured a Union artillery piece earning the respect of those seasoned veterans. The victory, however, was bittersweet for the cadets. The battle resulted in fifty-seven wounded and ten either killed in action or succumbing to their wounds afterwards, a casualty rate of over twenty percent.[17]

The Battle of New Market is a popular historical topic, and although many works briefly mention individual cadets, few know anything about the ten young men who gave their lives in the service of their school and state. The following is a brief biographical sketch of the ten cadets that "Died on the Field of Honor:"[18]

Samuel Francis Atwill. Born in Westmoreland County, Virginia on January 31, 1846, his parents were Samuel Bailey Atwill and Jane Ann Brown. Atwill matriculated at VMI in May of 1862 just prior to the end of the session. At the Battle of New Market, Atwill served as a corporal in Company A. During the battle he was "struck in the calf of the leg, his wound was considered severe, though not dangerous."[19] Moved to Staunton, Virginia after the battle to recuperate, during his convalescence he contracted lockjaw and died a most horrible death on July 20, 1864 at the home of Dr. F.T. Stribling. Atwill is one of the cadets interred beneath the New Market Battlefield

Figure 1. Samuel Atwell, c. 1863. Photograph, black and white print.

Monument at Virginia Military Institute.

William Henry Cabell. Cabell was born in Richmond, Virginia on November 13, 1845, the son of Dr. Robert Gamble Cabell and Margaret Caskie. His paternal grandfather, William H. Cabell was a Governor of Virginia. While a student at Richmond College in 1862, Cabell expressed an interest in joining the military. His father recommended that he plan for this future as a student at VMI. As advised, he matriculated at VMI in July of 1863, and fought (along with his brother Robert, a Cadet Private in Company A) as a Cadet 1st Sergeant in Company D. At the Battle of New Market, Cabell was "struck by a cannon-ball in the chest, [and] was left mortally wounded on the field of battle." Cabell was initially buried in New Market, but later his remains were disinterred and reburied in Hollywood Cemetery in Richmond.

Charles Gay Crockett. Crockett was born December 3, 1846 near Wytheville, Virginia, the son of Gustavus A. Crockett and Elizabeth E. Erskine. Crockett matriculated at VMI in February of 1864 and served as a private in Company D. Crockett died in the same artillery explosion that took the lives of William Cabell and Henry Jones. Crockett, like several other cadets, was first buried in New Market, but later laid to rest beneath the New Market Battlefield Monument at Virginia Military Institute.

Alva Curtis Hartsfield. Hartsfield was born June 5, 1844 in Wake County, North Carolina, the son of Wesley Hartsfield and Candace Smith. Hartsfield began his college education at the University of North Carolina, transferring to VMI in 1863 in the second class. He served in the Battle of New Market as a Cadet Private in Company B. Although wounded at New Market, Hartsfield went to Richmond with the remainder of the battalion. After collapsing in the streets of Petersburg, he was sent to a hospital in that city, where he died on June 26, 1864 as a result of the wounds received at New Market. He is buried in the Blandford Church Cemetery in Petersburg, Virginia.

Luther Cary Haynes. Haynes was born on February 11, 1845, the son of William Corbin Haynes and Maria Street. Haynes matriculated at VMI on November 10, 1863 and served as a Private in Company B at the Battle of New Market. After suffering a serious wound during the battle, he died June 5, 1864 at a hospital housed in the Powhatan Hotel in Richmond, Virginia. Cadet Haynes's remains rest at the family home in Essex County, VA in an unmarked grave.

Thomas Garland Jefferson. The son of John Garland Jefferson and Otelia Mansfield Howlett, Jefferson was born on January 1, 1846 in Amelia County, Virginia. Cadet Jefferson was the great-great nephew of President Thomas Jefferson. He matriculated at VMI on August 1, 1863 and served as a Private in Company B at the Battle of New Market. He suffered a mortal wound during the battle and died three days later, May 15 in New Market. When two members of his company stopped to try to give first aid, Jefferson pointed to the front and said, "You can do nothing for me; go to the front; there is the place for you."[20] Today, he rests beneath the New Market Monument at VMI.

Henry Jenner Jones. Jones was born on March 10, 1846 in King William County, Virginia. His parents were Thomas S. Jones and Mary E. (maiden name unknown). Jones served as a Private in Company D. Jones died, along with two other cadets, when a shell burst over their heads while charging the Union artillery. "His face lit up with the fire of battle, he fell ere his hand had been raised to avenge his own and his country's wrongs."[21] Along with some of his comrades, he is buried beneath the New Market Monument at VMI.

William Hugh McDowell. Cadet McDowell was born on December 31, 1846 in Iredell County, North Carolina. His parents were Robert Irwin McDowell and Rebekah Brevard. McDowell served as a Private in Company B. Killed in action at the Battle of New Market, McDowell is called the "Ghost Cadet" because of the fictional account of his participation in the Battle of New Market in *The Ghost Cadet*, an award-winning children's book by Elaine Marie Alphin. His remains lie beneath the New Market Battlefield Monument at VMI.

Figure 1. Cadet William H. McDowell, ambrotype, 1863.

Jaqueline Beverly Stanard. "Bev" was born in either 1844 or 1845, the son of Beverly Stanard and Ellen Taliaferro. Stanard first matriculated at VMI on January 20, 1863, but resigned on January 29, 1864. Eight days later, he was re-instated, and at the Battle of New Market he served as a Private in Company B. Stanard was one of three cadets killed by an artillery shell at the beginning of the cadet's advance. Stanard lived for a while and sent a message to his mother saying, "I fell where I wished to fall, fighting for my country, and I did not fight in vain. Tell my mother that I die with full confidence in my God."[22] He is buried in Graham Cemetery in Orange, Virginia.

Joseph Christopher Wheelwright. Born on September 26, 1846 in Westmoreland County, Virginia, the son of Dr. Frederick D. Wheelwright, and Maria L. (maiden name unknown), Wheelwright entered VMI in August of 1863 and served as a Private in Company C during the Battle of New Market. He suffered a mortal wound during the battle and died in Harrisonburg, Virginia on June 2, 1864. He rests beneath the New Market Monument at VMI.

For years the exploits of these ten young men, along with the others from the Virginia Military Institute who fought and bled at New Market, lived on in the memories of the veterans who fought with them, and in the imaginations of others who were not there. Eventually, the myths surrounding the cadets grew to such proportions that it was not just one gun that they captured, but an entire Union battery. The cadets' story became so famous that many seem to have forgotten the other five thousand men who fought with Breckenridge; the cadets seemed to have won the battle entirely by themselves. Sadly, the myths began to hide what the Corps of Cadets did accomplish. They fought as well as—and in some cases better than—many seasoned veterans; they held a critical position in a battle line that was weak, and they stood their ground and were in position to be in the lead during the final charge. While the myths tend to exaggerate the role the cadets played, there is no doubt that they were instrumental in the Confederate victory. The loss at New Market led to the reassignment of Sigel, and the return of General David Hunter, who would later remember the part the cadets played at New Market and take vengeance on their school.

When Hunter led his army through the Shenandoah Valley in June of 1864, he retaliated against Virginia Military Institute by burning and looting the campus. According to David Hunter Strother, General David Hunter's cousin and Chief of Staff, there were military reasons to burn the school. "The professors and cadets had taken the field against government troops, as an organized Corps. The buildings had been used as a Rebel arsenal and recently as a fortress."[23] Hunter's men pulled down and took away a bronze statue of George Washington on the campus. They looted and burned the library and laboratories. One Union officer noted, "The burning of the Institute made a grand picture, a vast volume of black smoke rolled above the flames and covered half the horizon."[24] The cadets, who had just returned to Lexington had to retreat, and could do nothing to prevent their beloved campus's devastation.

The extensive damage to all of the buildings as well as the loss of the library and laboratory equipment made closing the school necessary, and resulted in the furloughing of the Corps of Cadets. In his annual report on July 15, 1864, Superintendent Smith said, "Finding, upon examination, that most of our commissary stores had been destroyed or taken by the enemy—that the public property was in a state of utter ruin—I deemed it my duty to place all the cadets who were able to reach their homes, or the homes of their friends, on furlough."[25] It would be over a year before the cadets could return to their school.

An interesting footnote to the Battle of New Market and the burning of VMI occurred fifty years later. At the Battle of New Market, Henry DuPont was an artillery officer, and later reluctantly shelled VMI during Hunter's raid on Lexington. In 1914, DuPont was a senator from the State of Delaware and the sponsor of legislation compensating VMI for the damages sustained during the war. The Senate majority leader at that time was Senator Thomas Staples Martin of Virginia. Martin was a member of the VMI Corps of Cadets at the Battle of New Market.[26] Two men who fought bravely at New Market now worked together to help heal the wounds of war.

Notes

1. John Thomas Lewis Preston, *Historical Sketch of the Establishment and Organization of the Virginia Military Institute* (Lexington, VA: VMI Archives, 1889) 2-3.

2. James Lee Conrad, *The Young Lions: Confederate Cadets at War* (Mechanicsburg, PA: Stackpole Books, 1997), 1.

3. Ibid., 2.

4. Ibid., 3.

5. Conrad, 17.

6. Preston, 17-18.

7. Ibid., 33.

8. "The Execution of John Brown: Stonewall Jackson eyewitness Account," *VMI Archives*, accessed September 24, 2014, http://www.vmi.edu/archives.aspx?id-=4919.

9. Conrad, 41.

10. Ibid., 45.

11. Keith E. Gibson, "Virginia Military Institute at War," *Guide to Virginia's Civil War Battlefields and Sites*," accessed September 10, 2014, http://www.civilwartraveler.com/inprint/VCW-10-2-p1-2.pdf.

12. Michael G. Mahon, *The Shenandoah Valley, 1861-1865: The Destruction of the Granary of the Confederacy* (Mechanicsburg, PA: Stackpole Books, 1999), 108.

13. Scott H. Harris, "Put the Boys In": The Battle of New Market," accessed September 1, 2014, http://www.shenandoahatwar.org/The-History/The-Stories/Put-the-boys-in-The-Battle-of-New-Market.

14. Ibid.

15. Gibson, "Virginia Military Institute at War."

16. Mahon, 109.

17. William Couper, ed., *The Corps Forward: Biographical Sketches of the Cadets Who Fought in the Battle of New Market* (Charlottesville, VA: Mariner Press, 2005), 15.

18. The information contained in these biographies was compiled from several sources, including *The Corps Forward*, edited by William Couper, The VMI Archives, *Biographical Sketches of the Graduates and Eleves of the Virginia Military Institute Who Fell at the Battle of New Market* by Charles Walker, Find-A-Grave, and RootsWeb: Obituaries.

19. William Couper, ed., *The Corps Forward: Biographical Sketches of the Cadets Who Fought in the Battle of New Market* (Charlottesville, VA: Mariner Press, 2005), 15.

20. Charles D. Walker, *Biographical sketches of the Graduates and Eleves of the Virginia Military Institute who fell during the War Between the States (Philadelphia, PA: J.P. Lippincott, 1875),* 290.

21. Ibid., 311.

22. Ibid., 494.

23. David Hunter Strother, *A Virginia Yankee in the Civil War: The Diaries of David Hunter Strother* (Chapel Hill, NC: The University of North Carolina Press, 1961), 255.

24. "The Story of General David Hunter's 1864 Raid," *Hunter's Raid: The Lynchburg Campaign*, accessed September 15, 2014, http://www.huntersraid.org/story.html.

25. "The Burning of VMI, June 1864, From the Annual Report," *VMI Archives*, accessed September 15, 2014, http://www.vmi.edu/archives.aspx?id=4717.

26. "Heroism in Defeat," *Stone Sentinels*, accessed October 10, 2014, http://www.shenandoah.stonesentinels.com/New_Market/Heroism_in_Defeat.php.

Bibliography

Conrad, James Lee. *The Young Lions: Confederate Cadets at War*. Mechanicsburg, PA: Stackpole Books, 1997.

Couper, William, Editor. *The Corps Forward: Biographical Sketches of the Cadets Who Fought in the Battle of New Market*. Charlottesville, VA: Mariner Press, 2005.

Davis, William C. *The Battle of New Market*. Harrisburg, PA: Stackpole Books, 1993.

Davis, Julia. *A Valley and a Song: The Story of the Shenandoah River*. New York: Holt, Reinhart& Winston, 1963.

Editors of Time-Life Books. *The Shenandoah in Flames: The Valley Campaign of 1864*. Alexandria, VA: Time-Life Books, 1987.

Gibson, Keith E. "Virginia Military Institute at War," Guide to Virginia's Civil War Battlefields and Sites." Accessed September 10, 2014. http://www.civilwartraveler.com/inprint/VCW-10-2-p1-2.pdf.

Gindlesperger, James. *Seed Corn of the Confederacy: The Virginia Military Institute at New Market*. Shippensburg, PA: Burd Street Press, 1997.

"Heroism in Defeat." Stone Sentinels. Accessed October 10, 2014. http://www.shenandoah.stonesentinels.com/New_Market/Heroism_in_Defeat.php.

Knight, Charles R. *Valley Thunder: The Battle of New Market and the Opening of the Shenandoah Valley Campaign, May 1864*. El Dorado Hills, CA: Savas-Beatie, 2010.

Mahon, Michael G. *The Shenandoah Valley, 1861 – 1965: The Destruction of the Granary of the Confederacy*. Mechanicsburg, PA: Stackpole Books, 1999.

Preston, John Thomas Lewis. *Historical Sketch of the Establishment and Organization of the Virginia Military Institute*. Lexington, VA: VMI Archives, 1889.

Strother, David Hunter. *A Virginia Yankee in the Civil War: The Diaries of David Hunter Strother*. Chapel Hill, NC: University of North Carolina Press, 1961.

"The Burning of VMI, June 1864, From the Annual Report." *VMI Archives*. Accessed September 15, 2014. http://www.vmi.edu/archives.aspx?id=4717.

"The Execution of John Brown: Stonewall Jackson eyewitness Account." *VMI Archives*. Accessed September 24, 2014. http://www.vmi.edu/archives.aspx?id-=4919.

"The Story of General David Hunter's 1864 Raid." *Hunter's Raid: The Lynchburg Campaign*. Accessed September 15, 2014. http://www.huntersraid.org/story.html.

Turner, Edward Raymond. *The New Market Campaign, 1864*. Richmond, VA: Whittet &Shepperson, 1912.

Walker, Charles W. *Biographical sketches of the Graduates and Eleves of the Virginia Military Institute who fell during the War Between the States*. Philadelphia, PA: J.P. Lippincott, 1875.

The Air Zoo

Exhibit Review

Michael Majerczyk

The Air Zoo is an aviation museum located in Portage, Michigan on the southwest side of the Lower Peninsula. The museum features two campuses, the Main Campus and the East Campus. In all, the Air Zoo has fifty aircraft on display. In the main exhibit hall, one can view perennial favorites such as the SR-71 Blackbird, B-25 Mitchell, P-47 Thunderbolt, and F-14 Tomcat. The lighting in the main exhibit hall is somewhat low but better and more interesting than the lighting at the National Museum of the USAF in Dayton, Ohio. Thus, it is wise to bring along a camera tripod and museum officials do not object to this. The Air Zoo placed colored lights in strategic positions to give interesting color effects to the aircraft on display. For example, when viewed from the right hand side, the SR-71 takes on an interesting gold hue.

Figure 1: SR-71 Blackbird. All photos taken by the author with a tripod mounted Sony A-6000, Minolta MC Rokkor 28 mm lens and remote shutter release.

In addition to jet fighters, the Air Zoo has a considerable collection of bi-planes. Nevertheless, the focus of this review is on World War II aircraft, in particular, the two SBD Dauntless dive-bombers the museum has on display. The core of the Air Zoo's WWII fighter aircraft is located in the Main Campus in its own wing adjacent to a considerable collection of WW II artifacts. Here, in addition to others, visitors can view the FG-1D Corsair, F6F-5 Hellcat, FM-2 Wildcat, and SBD-3 Dauntless. The lighting here is bright and it is clear by the absence of dust, and the near polished finish on the aircraft, that they are well kept. Nevertheless, space in this wing is at a premium and it is difficult, though not impossible, to get a good shot of a few of the exhibits with one's camera. Still, the limited space allows the visitor to get inches from the aircraft. This provides a more personal connection to favorites such as the Corsair and Dauntless.

The East Campus is within walking distance of the Main Campus. The East Campus includes an impressive display of engines. They include the Allison V-1710 that powered such aircraft as the P-40 Warhawk, the Pratt & Whitney R-2800 that powered the Corsair, and the famous Rolls Royce Merlin that powered, amongst others, the Supermarine Spitfire and the P-51 Mustang. The most notable feature of this display is that the engines are not behind glass. That is, the visitor

Figure 2. This image shows a section of the Allison V-1710 valve train. The Allison used a single overhead cam with four valves per cylinder. Ford Motor Company was the prime supplier of the R-2800 and they produced the engine in Dearborn, Michigan. Additionally, Continental Motors Corporation built the Merlin under license from Rolls Royce in Muskegon, Michigan.

can walk right up to the engines as if they were sitting on an engine stand in one's garage.

Because glare is not an issue, one can expect an enhanced viewing experience and photographic opportunities. This is well in contrast to the engines displayed at the Smithsonian National Air and Space Museum. There, engines are enclosed in glass and in some cases, they are cordoned off leaving significant space between the engine and the visitors. At the Air Zoo, one can peer directly into the valve train of the Allison V-1710 free of glass or border ropes.

Additional bi-planes are on display on the East Campus but the most impressive feature is the workshop where the restoration of two planes is underway, a Dauntless dive-bomber and a Wildcat fighter. Recovery teams pulled these two planes—along with the Dauntless displayed on the main campus—from the bottom of Lake Michigan.

To provide training for new pilots during WWII, Lake Michigan was home to two makeshift aircraft carriers, the *USS Wolverine* and *USS Sable*. These ships began life as the Great Lakes passenger ships *SS Seaandbee* and *SS Greater Buffalo*.[1] The Detroit Shipbuilding Company in Wyandotte, Michigan, built the *SS Seaandbee* in 1913 and the American Ship Building Company, Lorain, Ohio, and Great Lakes Engineering Works, Ecorse, Michigan, worked to realize the *SS Greater Buffalo*. Both ships used coal-fired boilers and side-wheel propulsion. The *USS Wolverine's* name paid tribute to the state of Michigan where workers originally built the ship and to Lake Michigan where she would operate.[2] American Shipbuilding at Buffalo converted both ships. *The USS Wolverine* received her

Figure 3. The *USS Wolverine*. Source: http://www.sheboyganpress.com/story/life/2015/06/12/sheboygan-history/71153346/

commission in 1942 and the *USS Sable* in early 1943. Both the *USS Wolverine* and the *USS Sable's* homeport was Chicago's Navy Pier.[3]

The Great Lakes were free of enemy ships and submarines. Thus, neither the *USS Wolverine* nor the *USS Sable* were fitted with armor or weapons. This provided both the ships' crew and the pilots some measure of comfort. Nevertheless, accidents occurred. Of the 116,000 landings made on these ships, only 120 pilots ditched their plane or crashed into Lake Michigan.[4]

The SBD-3 Dauntless BuNo. 00624 on display at the Main Campus of the Air Zoo rested on the bottom of Lake Michigan for fifty years. Once recovered, restoration technicians, staff, and volunteers at the Air Zoo spent nine years bringing the plane to show condition. Flying from the *USS Ranger,* BuNo. 00624 took part in Operation Torch, the invasion of North Africa in 1942. Lieutenant John "Jacko" DeVane Jr., awarded the Navy Cross, logged most of BuNo. 00624's flight time.[5]

Figure 4. SBD-3 Dauntless BuNo. 00624. Note the perforated braking flaps. These slowed the plane's dive and provided the pilot with increased maneuverability. Photo taken by the author.

The second Dauntless on display at the Air Zoo, SBD-2p 2173, is still undergoing restoration. Though its history is unclear, BuNo 2173 was likely present at the Battle of Coral Sea aboard the USS Yorktown. In 1944, perhaps due to carburetor icing, BuNo. 2173's engine cut out during a training run. The pilot, Lieutenant John Lendo, ditched the plane in Lake Michigan. A and T Recovery pulled the plane from 250 feet of water in 2009.[6]

Figure 5. SBD-2p BuNo. 2137. Visitors can stand shoulder to shoulder with the restoration technicians at the Air Zoo. Photo by the author.

Figure 6. SBD-2p BuNo. 2137. Photo by the author.

The Dautless's proudest moment came in 1942 during the Battle of Midway. Excellent intelligence proved instrumental to the victory at Midway. Concerning ships allotted to the battle, the Japanese Navy held the advantage. However, airpower was much more even. Three American carriers, the *USS Yorktown*, *USS Hornet,* and *USS Enterprise* had the additional benefit of the airfield on Midway island to provide air power. This matched up well to Vice Admiral Chuichi Nagumo's four carriers, the *Akagi*, *Kaga*, *Soryu*, and *Hiryu*.[7] The advantage Admiral Nimitz had was that he knew the Japanese were coming. Thus, he planned to ambush the Japanese fleet. *The USS Hornet* and *USS Enterprise* laid in wait north of Midway at a position named Point Luck.[8] Commander C.W. McClusky departed *Enterprise* with thirty-three Dauntless dive-bombers. When McClusky arrived at the coordinates, the Japanese fleet was not there. McClusky received incorrect information. He made the decision to continue on his heading for another thirty-five miles, then turn to starboard, and follow the last known heading of the Japanese fleet until fuel consumption forced him back to *Enterprise*.[9]

With five minutes remaining before he had to return to *Enterprise*, McClusky's two squadrons of Dauntless dive bombers crossed paths with the Japanese destroyer *Arashi* on its way to regroup with the Japanese carrier fleet after depth charging maneuvers against American submarines. McClusky adjusted to the destroyer's heading and ten minutes later, he found the Japanese fleet.[10] Flying TBD Devastator torpedo planes, an earlier attack by Torpedo Eight from *USS Hornet* and Torpedo Six from *USS Enterprise* had Japanese defenses trained low.[11] This allowed McClusky and his two squadrons along with Max Leslie's Bombing Three from *USS Yorktown* arriving from the south to dive on the Japanese fleet with little opposition.[12] Furthermore, munitions and refueling planes covered the flight decks of the Japanese carriers. Leslie's group totaled seventeen dive-bombers. Due to engine difficulties, one of McClusky's pilots had to turn back, leaving thirty-two. Nevertheless, in a span of five minutes, dive-bombers hit and mortally wounded the *Akagi*, *Kaga,* and *Soryu*.[13] Later that afternoon, Bombing Six, Bombing Three, and Scouting Six from *Enterprise*, flying twenty-five Dauntlesses, scored hits on the remaining carrier *Hiryu*.[14] She sank the next day.

A visit to the Air Zoo brings the machines pilots such as C.W. McClusky flew up close and personal. Events such as the Battle of Midway are riveting—and indeed, so is the attention to detail restoration technicians at the Air Zoo employ. Though it is not as big as the National Museum of the USAF or the Smithsonian Air and Space Museum, the Air Zoo's inviting setting surrounding all the exhibits makes for a welcoming visit and makes up for any shortcomings.

SBD-3 Dauntless Specifications

Design	Specifications
Crew	Two: Pilot and Gunner
Wingspan	Forty-one feet six inches
Engine	Wright R-1820-32
Power	1000 hp
Top Speed	250 mph
Max Bomb Load	1,200 pounds
Pilot's armament	Two fixed 50.s
Gunner's armament	Two movable 30.s

Table 1. Specifications. Source: Appendix B. Barrett Tillman, *The Dive Bombers of World War Two.*

Notes

1. Paul M. Somers, *Lake Michigan Aircraft Carriers* (Charleston S.C: Arcadia, 2003),19,43.

2. Ibid., 60.

3. Beth Dippel, "Sheboygan County History: Aircraft Carriers Once Roamed Lake Michigan," Sheboygan Press Media, June 12, 2015, accessed December 31, 2016, http://www.sheboyganpress.com/story/life/2015/06/12/sheboygan-history/71153346/

4. Ibid.

5. SBD-3 Dauntless, Information taken from the placard at the Air Zoo on December 29, 2016.

6. SBD-2p Dauntless, Information taken from the placard at the Air Zoo on December 29,2016.

7. Harald L. Buell, *Dauntless Helldivers* (New York: Orion, 1986),81; Barrett Tillman, *The Dauntless Dive Bomber of World War Two* (Annapolis: Naval Institute, 1976), 60.

8. Buell, 83.

9. Tillman, 70.

10. Ibid.

11. Stephen L. Moore, Pacific Payback, *The Carrier Aviators Who Avenged Pearl Harbor at the Battle of Midway* (New York: Caliber, 2003), 185, 190.

12. Tillman, 74.

13. Moore, 212.

14. Tillman, 84.

Bibliography

Buell, Harold L. *Dauntless Helldiver*. New York: Orion, 1986.

Dippel, Beth. "Sheboygan County History: Aircraft Carriers Once Roamed Lake Michigan." Sheyboygan Press Media, Accessed January 4, 2017. http://www.sheboyganpress.com/story/life/2015/06/12/sheboygan-history/71153346/

Moore, Stephen L. *Pacific Payback: The Carrier Aviators Who Avenged Pearl Harbor At The Battle Of Midway*. New York: NAL Caliber, 2015.

Somers, Paul M. *Lake Michigan Aircraft Carriers*. Charleston S.C: Arcadia, 2003.

Tillman, Barrett. *The Dauntless Dive Bomber of World War Two*. Annapolis: Naval Institute, 1976.

Paul Andrew Hutton, *The Apache Wars: The Hunt for Geronimo, the Apache Kid, and the Captive Boy Who Started the Longest War in American History,* 2016.
Book Review

Stan Prager

There were once millions of Amerindians in North America. These diverse cultures spoke a wide variety of languages and belonged to hundreds of tribes and countless clans. European pandemics decimated these populations at contact, while the introduction of horses, firearms, and alcohol irrevocably altered traditional lifeways for a continent-wide distribution of native peoples that pursued vastly different strategies in diverse environments. They had little in common except in the eyes of the white invaders who viewed them as an impediment to expansion, colonization, and domination. Anthropologist Russel Thornton has estimated that by 1800 there were only six hundred thousand Native Americans left; by the 1890s, this number was a mere two hundred fifty thousand, about four to five percent of the pre-contact population.[1] By that time, none of them lived free in their traditional societies. Today, most Americans only know of these largely extinct peoples from their caricatures as noble savages or bloodthirsty villains in the largely

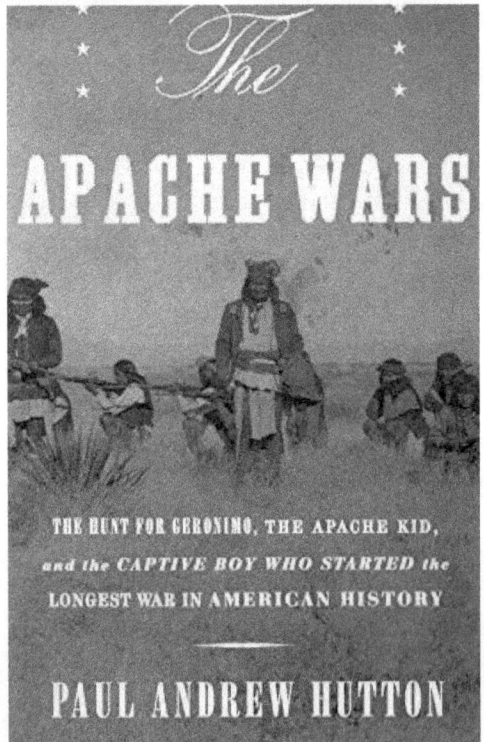

Figure 1. Cover art, used by permission of Paul Andrew Hutton.

mythical universe of the classic Hollywood Western. Thus, it is especially welcome to come to Paul Andrew Hutton's stirring historical narrative, *The Apache Wars: The Hunt for Geronimo, the Apache Kid, and the Captive Boy Who Started the Longest War in American History*, which resurrects the actual people and events, and way of life, so long buried in fanciful myth.[2]

Population pressures had once driven a loose coalition of peoples known as Apaches into the Southwest. Like many native peoples, they operated without central authority. Despite relationships that implied far more significance to European observers than it did to them, tribes and clans occupied different geographies with diverse lifeways and were frequently hostile to one another with deeply embedded blood feuds. There were six major Apache-speaking groups: Chiricahua, Jicarilla, Lipan, Mescalero, Plains Apache, and Western Apache, with many sub-groups and clans within these, all politically autonomous. Some of them made their way by raiding the settled agricultural peoples on both sides of the border between Mexico and the United States territories that later would become Arizona and New Mexico. They stole cattle, horses, and even people to be sold into slavery. For the Apache, as Hutton underscores, raiding was distinct from warfare. There were sometimes casualties as a by-product of raids, but killing was not the intention.

Yet, Hutton, professor of history at the University of New Mexico and the executive director of Western History Association, does not romanticize his subjects. The Apache were fearsome and often brutal warriors, who frequently tortured their prisoners to death in horrific ways, such as staking them to anthills with their mouths propped open, flaying them alive, suspending them upside down with hot coals beneath their heads,[3] and tying them to burning wagons.[4] Apaches were also sometimes known for murdering women and children, even in one report shooting down a pregnant woman with a baby in her arms and then bashing the infant's head against a wall.[5] But they had no monopoly on barbarism. Mexicans and Americans alike often reacted to the misdeeds of a single clan or even a lone Apache by slaughtering unrelated bands of men, women, and children in retaliation.

The Apache Wars is a long, complicated, yet generally fast-moving narrative of how random clashes between Apaches and American settlers in the Southwest ignited a lengthy, vicious conflict and ultimately ended up with the virtual annihilation of the Apache and the deportation of pockets of survivors. It began with the unlikely spark of the kidnapping of a red-haired one-eyed boy. Felix Ward, "the Captive Boy" in the subtitle, was the child of a Mexican woman and adopted son of a white settler whose ranch Apache raiders preyed upon. Raised by Indians and later known as Mickey Free, he grew up to be an amoral Apache scout in service of the U.S. Cavalry. As the book's protagonist, he is emblematic of the phantom potential for assimilation among hostile forces that never really could be. Because whites often viewed all Indians through a single lens, they frequently randomly punished Apaches that settled into peaceful lifeways as severely as those who continued to raid. Likewise, to those who refused to capitulate, they reviled the "White Eyes" as a single indistinguishable force. Of course, a history of ongoing treachery by whites fueled this hatred. Invited to a parlay by the cavalry, the legendary Cochise barely escaped assassination.[6] Soldiers took the great chief Mangas Coloradas prisoner, then taunted and executed him. He was scalped, and then his head was boiled so the skull could be taken as trophy, later gifted to a famed phrenologist.[7] Soldiers also executed without cause the famous mystic, Nock-ay-det-klinne, known as "the Dreamer," although he had preached peace.[8] Whites violated every agreement made with the Apaches, and as elsewhere in the expanding nation, natives humbled in reservations fared no better than those who would fight to the last warrior.

There were whites who were sympathetic to the Apache cause, including the famous scout Kit Carson, frontiersman Tom "Taglito" Jeffords, and Civil War General O. O. Howard. These were a distinct minority. Some, like Indian agent John Clum, began with humanitarian ideals that sought to improve the often-deplorable conditions on reservations. But ego and ambition got the better of him, and he failed to recognize the inherent inhumanity in what were essentially internment camps that proved to be breeding grounds for disease and drunkenness. Nor did he account for the explosive nature of settling hostile tribes juggling long-simmering blood feuds within the same geography. His intentions hardly averted the disaster that his efforts were to spawn. Others, like General George Crook, took a more brutal approach yet did not do so out of unclean motives; the Apache scouts that Mickey Free joined as a wing of the cavalry was a Crook innovation. Still, most whites—soldiers and settlers alike—simply sought the extermination of the Apache and showed little reluctance in their single-minded pursuit of that goal.

What brings great beauty to The Apache Wars is the tapestry of anecdotal tales that enhance the narrative. Two are especially symbolic. In the first, the reader learns that Agent Clum had created a tribal police force at his San Carlos reservation, and that a chief named Des-a-lin, angry at a public rebuke from Clum,

> [F]ound Clum in his office and attempted to shoot him but was instead shot dead by his own brother—the police officer Tauelclyee. As the two men looked down at Des-a-lin's body, Tauelclyee absentmindedly stroked his smoking rifle and said:

"I have killed my own chief and my own brother. But he was trying to kill you, and 1 am a policeman. It was my duty." Clum warmly clasped his hand and assured the distraught man that what he had done was right, and that they would remain forever brothers and friends.[9]

The second chronicles the tragic attempts of Aravaipa chief Eskiminzin to cement peace with the whites, as he is twice betrayed and his people massacred.

> Eskiminzin rode to a nearby ranch owned by Charles McKinney, a thirty-five-year-old Irish im-migrant . . . McKinney had long been a friend to Eskiminzin . . . The Irishman invited his old friend in to supper, and after dinner they sat together on the porch to smoke and talk of the troubling times. When the last smoke was put out, Eskiminzin rose, thanked his friend for his hospitality, pulled his revolver, and shot him dead at point-blank range. He then rode off into the mountains. "I did it to teach my people that there must be no friendship between them and the white man," Eskiminzin sadly explained. "Anyone can kill an enemy, but it takes a strong man to kill a friend."[10]

There is little tedium in Hutton's exciting narrative, punctuated with much color and a plethora of blood and tears on both sides. The famous Geronimo has a central role in the story, and tragically, whites afforded all Apaches disproportionate punishment in retaliation for his depredations, both real and imagined, although he was indeed an especially cruel and brutal fellow. In the end too, all Apaches paid the price for being indigenous Native Americans in the way of white colonizers, first forced into reservations in often dehumanizing conditions, and then deported vast distances from their homeland in order to make way for more white settlements. Apache scouts assisting the cavalry, tribal police forces, peaceful reservation Indians—none fared any better and most fared far worse than the murderous Geronimo, who was to unpredictably ride in President Theodore Roosevelt's 1905 inaugural parade and to die an old man who long outlived the events that made him infamous.

A careful read does detect some flaws: it is possible but unlikely that all of the significant female characters were in fact "beautiful," as Hutton reports. And there may have been some overreach in his efforts to tie a number of well-known key events to his narrative, as he does in his attempt to link hostilities here with the birth of the Pony Express, which is likely stretching it a bit.[11] But these are no more than quibbles in what otherwise deserves large measures of praise.

As Americans of the twenty-first century try to come to grips with the mass extermination of the aboriginal peoples that were the original occupants of these lands, it is instructive to look to the existential sentiment attributed to General Phillip Sheridan—who makes an appearance in The Apache Wars—that "The only good Indian is a dead Indian." This was a surprisingly common doctrine among Americans of that era, even by allegedly more enlightened thinkers like Theodore Roosevelt. Although he later included Geronimo in his inaugural parade, Roosevelt nevertheless plucked that theme with great vigor in an 1886 speech when he said that "I don't go so far as to think that the only good Indians are the dead Indians, but I believe nine out of every 10 are . . . And I shouldn't like to inquire too closely into the case of the tenth."[12] The Apache Wars is a blueprint for how this conviction effected an obliteration of an entire people in just one corner of the United States.

The author previously published a slightly different version of this review of *The Apache Wars: The Hunt for Geronimo, the Apache Kid, and the Captive Boy Who Started the Longest War in American History* on his book blog at https://regarp.com/2016/11/24/review-of-the-apache-wars-the-hunt-for-geronimo-the-apache-kid-and-the-captive-boy-who-started-the-longest-war-in-american-history-by-paul-andrew-hutton/

Notes

1. Russel Thornton, *American Indian Holocaust and Survival: A Population History Since 1492* (Norman, OK: University of Oklahoma Press, 1990), 43, accessed November 24, 2016, Google Books.

2. Paul Andrew Hutton, *The Apache Wars: The Hunt for Geronimo, the Apache Kid, and the Captive Boy Who Started the Longest War in American History* (NY: Crown Publishing, 2016, uncorrected proof edition).

3. Ibid., 12.

4. Ibid., 47.

5. Ibid., 374.

6. Ibid., 42.

7. Ibid., 101-02.

8. Ibid., 280.

9. Ibid., 196.

10. Ibid., 140-41.

11. Ibid., 58-59.

12. Alysa Landry, "Theodore Roosevelt: 'The Only Good Indians Are the Dead Indians,'" *Indian Country Media Network* (June 28, 2016), accessed November 23, 2016, https://indiancountrymedianetwork.com/history/events/theodore-roosevelt-the-only-good-indians-are-the-dead-indians/.

Featured Titles from Westphalia Press

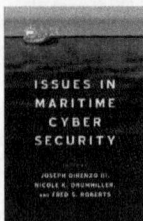

Issues in Maritime Cyber Security Edited by Nicole K. Drumhiller, Fred S. Roberts, Joseph DiRenzo III and Fred S. Roberts

While there is literature about the maritime transportation system, and about cyber security, to date there is very little literature on this converging area. This pioneering book is beneficial to a variety of audiences looking at risk analysis, national security, cyber threats, or maritime policy.

The Death Penalty in the Caribbean: Perspectives from the Police Edited by Wendell C. Wallace PhD

Two controversial topics, policing and the death penalty, are skillfully interwoven into one book in order to respond to this lacuna in the region. The book carries you through a disparate range of emotions, thoughts, frustrations, successes and views as espoused by police leaders throughout the Caribbean

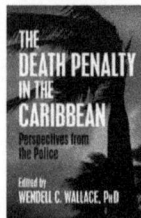

Middle East Reviews: Second Edition Edited by Mohammed M. Aman PhD and Mary Jo Aman MLIS

The book brings together reviews of books published on the Middle East and North Africa. It is a valuable addition to Middle East literature, and will provide an informative read for experts and non-experts on the MENA countries.

Unworkable Conservatism: Small Government, Freemarkets, and Impracticality by Max J. Skidmore

Unworkable Conservatism looks at what passes these days for "conservative" principles—small government, low taxes, minimal regulation—and demonstrates that they are not feasible under modern conditions.

The Politics of Impeachment Edited by Margaret Tseng

This edited volume addresses the increased political nature of impeachment. It is meant to be a wide overview of impeachment on the federal and state level, including: the politics of bringing impeachment articles forward, the politicized impeachment proceedings, the political nature of how one conducts oneself during the proceedings and the political fallout afterwards.

Demand the Impossible: Essays in History as Activism
Edited by Nathan Wuertenberg and William Horne

Demand the Impossible asks scholars what they can do to help solve present-day crises. The twelve essays in this volume draw inspiration from present-day activists. They examine the role of history in shaping ongoing debates over monuments, racism, clean energy, health care, poverty, and the Democratic Party.

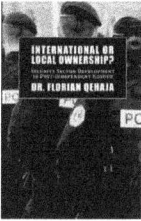

International or Local Ownership?: Security Sector Development in Post-Independent Kosovo
by Dr. Florian Qehaja

International or Local Ownership? contributes to the debate on the concept of local ownership in post-conflict settings, and discussions on international relations, peacebuilding, security and development studies.

Donald J. Trump's Presidency: International Perspectives
Edited by John Dixon and Max J. Skidmore

President Donald J. Trump's foreign policy rhetoric and actions become more understandable by reference to his personality traits, his worldview, and his view of the world. As such, his foreign policy emphasis was on American isolationism and economic nationalism.

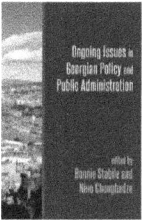

Ongoing Issues in Georgian Policy and Public Administration
Edited by Bonnie Stabile and Nino Ghonghadze

Thriving democracy and representative government depend upon a well functioning civil service, rich civic life and economic success. Georgia has been considered a top performer among countries in South Eastern Europe seeking to establish themselves in the post-Soviet era.

Poverty in America: Urban and Rural Inequality and Deprivation in the 21st Century
Edited by Max J. Skidmore

Poverty in America too often goes unnoticed, and disregarded. This perhaps results from America's general level of prosperity along with a fairly widespread notion that conditions inevitably are better in the USA than elsewhere. Political rhetoric frequently enforces such an erroneous notion.

westphaliapress.org